TREAT YOURSELF TO LIFE

TREAT YOURSELF TO LIFE

REVISED AND UPDATED EDITION

Raymond Charles Barker

 DeVorss *Publications*

ISBN: 0-87516-700-4
Library of Congress Card Catalog No.: 87-30216

First DeVorss Edition, 1996

DeVorss & Company, Publisher
P.O. Box 550
Marina del Rey, CA 90294

Printed in The United States of America

Contents

1

Treat Yourself to Happiness

"WILL I EVER be happy again?" is the cry which comes from the hearts of thousands.

For fifty years I have been talking with many hundreds of these people and have proved to them that their happiness can be regained and expanded IF they follow a few simple rules.

Wherever you are, in an apartment in New York or San Francisco, a farm in Iowa, a house in Texas or a bungalow in Florida, there is an inner you which is craving love, self-expression, permanence in your health and security in money.

If not actually fearful of the future, you are at best suffering mild anxiety, the number one mental symptom of the twentieth century.

Elizabeth Andrews in a great New York City hospital looked up at me from her bed and said:

"I have just been told by the doctors that I have Padgett's Disease, a malignant disease, and that I will never walk again without heavy braces and crutches. I don't want to accept this verdict. Need I?"

Knowing that this woman was capable of making drastic changes in her thinking and feeling, I answered:

"While the factual evidence of bone disease is true—your need to believe it permanent is not. You can treat yourself out of this, and I know it can be done."

Eight months later, without a brace or a crutch, Elizabeth Andrews walked into her church on a Sunday morning and joined others in the acknowledgement of a Power which knows no incurability!

How could this happen? Life limits no one, offers itself freely to all. If you can accept this new viewpoint as Elizabeth did, you can treat yourself to greater living. Elizabeth had learned that what man, with his material science, could not do for her, creative thinking could, provided she directed it herself.

Standing at her bedside on the day of her sentence to a life of invalidism, I saw her faint hope that I would agree she would walk again. Knowing her sincerity, and her capacity in the past to control her thinking, I immediately said:

"You certainly can walk again, and I will help you every step of the way."

Every day for months, she and I knew certain basic truths together. She, in her hospital bed, and I, in my home or office, replaced in her subconscious the verdict of an incurable disease with a sure knowledge of a woman walking through life with ease.

One cold autumnal day when Elizabeth was walking down Fifth Avenue, she suddenly fell. The ambulance interne told her she had broken her leg. Her fall, however, had not been the usual kind, no broken pavement, no icy sidewalk, nothing to trip over. The bones in her right leg had simply given way!

At the hospital the X-Rays showed the disease. The doctor anxiously made his way to her room, carrying the pictures with him, hoping that as her own eyes saw the condition, the blow would be softened as he told her: "You have Padgett's Disease."

She had faith in her doctor and obeyed his orders. She knew that his diagnosis was accurate and factual.

For a single moment the news terrified her, tears came to her eyes and panic clutched her heart. But she instantly turned in thought to her greater faith in God and affirmed that the Creative Power was equal to this situation. The calm came, the faith returned, and I came to her bedside in answer to her call.

Her recovery was not miraculous. For four months she never left the bed. I was there the day they brought to her the heavy massive brace, to cover her from hip to toe. She looked at it and had a momentary cry. Then, catching herself, she turned to me and said:

"We'll fool them yet, won't we?" My agreement with her faith was instantaneous.

Four months later she walked into church without that brace or even a crutch!

The key to Elizabeth's victory was in her own ability to keep her thinking clear and to waver not in her knowledge of her own self as a creative channel for an unlimited intelligence. She knew that life would respond to her as she responded to it.

This reciprocal action between your patterns of thought and feeling, and the universal life has determined every experience which you have ever had, are having or will ever have.

You can learn how to treat yourself to greater living. Your mind is no different than Elizabeth's, mine or anyone's else. The greatest sages, saints and messiahs had minds no greater and no finer than yours. Only, they knew how to use them. They knew how to keep their minds directed to creative ends. This book is not written to give you faith, that your church will give you. It is written to show you how to translate your faith into right subconscious action, to produce the results you want.

You are producing in life only a fraction of what you really want. You watch the few achieve, and then you alibi yourself into the docility of failure. Life takes you at your own evaluation. God has never limited man, and doesn't limit you. In fact, every religious system has proclaimed that God is always inspiring you to greater and finer achievements. If God is for you, then you had better be for yourself.

Your mind determines your experience. Your thinking and feeling nature is the cause of your experience. This statement no longer needs to be proved. Psychology, medicine and modern religion are implying this and are gathering continual evidence of its validity. Old forms of prayer are disappearing. New forms are revealing that the universe is an unlimited field for personal exploration.

Gone are the negative beseechings to a distant power. Today great masses of people are aware that the nature of life as you live it, here and now, has within itself the creative power of accomplishment. But only those who dare to emerge from the accepted beliefs of the crowd can prove this. Before reading further, you had better realize that your results will be determined by your ability to let go of the past, to realize the greatness of the moment, and to accept for yourself increased good in the future.

Your future is self-determined. You may not believe this,

but it is true. I have spent fifty years listening to people who tried to convince me how sick they were, how poor and unhappy they were, or how unappreciated they were. Always they have declared that the cause of their problem came from sources outside themselves. It is easier to blame the weather for your cold than it is to realize that your unconscious anger has produced it. It is easier to blame your partner for an unhappy marriage than it is to ask yourself: "In the last five years have I been the kind of a person with whom another could live happily?"

People in problems give more than sixty per cent of their thinking, feeling and talking to the details of their problem. Suggest to a chronic complainer that he change his attitudes and his topics of conversation. You will soon realize why he is where he is, experiencing what he is. To the observer the facts fit together, the cause is obvious and the correction is possible. To the sufferer with his whole thought absorbed in his condition, the remarks of a helpful friend are meaningless.

There are four major fields of experience in life. Actually, you can have only four basic problems, health, wealth, love and self-expression. You think of these problems as sickness, lack of money, unhappy personal relationships or frustration in your work. You may have one or two of these or any combination of them.

Whatever you think your lack may be, you are probably at this moment concentrating on it, and giving it your complete attention. Yet you are constantly disappointed that you do not have an abundance of health, love, money and creative self-expression. You say in chagrin:

"Must my present life be so incomplete?"

No, you did not come into this world to be unhappy. Life wants you to be happy, healthy and fulfilled. The way you can be happy and fulfilled in these four areas of your experience is to treat yourself to life.

Elizabeth Andrews' seemingly miraculous recovery from a malignant disease was a result of her practice of scientific prayer, called treatment.

What is treatment? I define it as using your conscious mind to select what you want, and next directing your sub-conscious mind to bring this into objective experience.

This method of prayer is the spiritual technique now being used successfully by men, women, and even children, to transform their conscious desires into objective reality, through directing the subconscious mind.

That is treatment.
It is simple.
It is concrete.
It is practical.
A power is in you right at this instant waiting to be released into the creative action which is your natural birthright, whether it is in your own health, your relations with other people, or your own work.

All the love there is in the world is in you and around you at this instant.
It is waiting only for the release that comes through your active awareness of it.

All the health there is in the world is yours at this instant.
It is waiting only for the revelation of the perfect man covered by the ailing man.

All the riches you need in the world are yours at this instant.
They await only your acceptance.

The creative drive you have always had is now in action.
It is calling and waiting for you to let it out into the world, to let it shine before a world that will receive you with love,

warmth and joy, since you and creation are one, inseparable and eternal.

You may want better health as Elizabeth did; or marriage, more friends, a finer home, or a career which gives you self-expression. Whatever it is you want, you can bring it into your experience now, if you will realize that you can treat yourself to that experience.

Psychiatrists and psychologists for eighty years have plumbed the depths of the subconscious to help patients to self-awareness. This has been sufficient therapy in many cases. These psychological techniques, however, lack a spiritual premise with which to bring the patient's desires for happiness into real experience.

The method I have taught thousands of men and women, namely treatment, takes up where the psychologists leave off. Self-awareness plus self-treatment results in a demonstration of whatever you want in life. That is my conviction after fifty years' teaching.

The technique of treatment is not merely for problem-ridden people; it is for all who wish richer living in the four major areas of human experience.

The basis of treatment is that your subconscious mind is a part of the mind of God. Your subconscious mind is your best friend, your creator, your ally. It will go to work for you at this instant to produce all the joy, all the love, all the peace in your world that you can possibly want. Being a part of the infinite mind, it plays the leading role in the creative process. It is that part of the universal mind which is a law as unchanging and unrelenting as the law of gravity.

Let's discuss this law. The law in any science is merely a definition of the way it works, of the way things happen. When we speak of the law of gravity, we are not describing a person, a place, a thing or even a sensation. We are describing an operation of law that is mathematically accurate. If you let go of this book, it will drop to the floor. Not because you want it to drop or do not want it to drop, but because a law causes it to drop.

The law of mind is the automatic action of the subconscious. We neither start it, stop it, increase it, decrease it nor do anything else to it. It is law. You can pray from now to doomsday for the suspension of the law of gravity but it will not take place. It cannot; it is the way it is.

This is also true of the law of mind. The subconscious is more than a storehouse of neuroses, psychoses, fixations, memories and habits. It is a law of action. It is a law in the sense that it is the way you and I work. It is the thing that causes you to be yourself. Treatment is the consistent repetition of a positive idea directed to your subconscious mind which is a part of the universal mind.

You condition your subconscious through treatment. This is not the Coué system which was taught years ago. In those days people were told that thoughts were things and all they needed to do was to think optimistically and positively and everything would be all right. A great many people tried this. They went around smiling and bearing their problems. But things did not turn out all right. We know today that a surface mind optimism will not cure a deeply disturbed pattern in the subconscious.

There is a science of prayer. Psychologists have their depth psychology with a human mind therapy. I am teaching a depth religion, with a spiritual therapy called treatment.

Think good thoughts, yes; but realize that good thoughts on the surface with a nasty disposition below the surface are merely another coat of paint on the same old house. The fresh paint on the old house does not make it a new house; it merely makes it attractive. There are unfortunately a great many people with attractive surface attitudes but with the same old rubbish underneath.

Elizabeth Andrews could never have been cured of malignant disease by the law of mind, had she merely believed in her conscious mind that it was possible. Not until Elizabeth had a subconscious conviction that she was a perfect spiritual being could she be healed. The medical profession did everything it could do for her. I worked with Elizabeth consistently, using treatment to transform her spiritual perfection into physical wholeness.

At this point I want to clarify the difference between prayer, meditation and treatment. When I use the word prayer, I think of it as an action on the part of man, reaching out to a God in order to get something. The word prayer indicates petition or asking. This is the customary procedure. You are asking a Deity for something, on the basis that you don't already have it. I believe you already have it; therefore you don't have to ask for it!

Meditation, the second method, is the act of absorbing an idea into consciousness. As you meditate upon an idea you absorb it into the structure of your thought, and it becomes you. Meditation is a quiet, relaxed absorption of ideas. The difference between meditation and treatment is absorption. In prayer you beg for an idea. In meditation you absorb an idea. In treatment you project an idea. They are quite different. Meditation has been practiced by the prophets and the saints of the ages. They learned to be still; they learned to relax. They experienced an interior communion with great ideas of truth. They assimilated these ideas which then became a working part of their own mental structure.

Prayer and meditation differ greatly from treatment. Treatment is dynamic thinking of God and His manifestations. Treatment is the act on the part of the individual wherein he thinks as God thinks, and God always thinks dynamically. Treatment is the synchronization of the individual with the universal mind. It is the blending of the individual with the universal, so that the individual merely becomes the vehicle through which the universal acts, and the individual can direct that action to a given end.

Meditation may be more or less aimless, but treatment is always specific mental action to a definite end. In meditation you might meditate on the idea that God is love. You relax and take that thought into your mind. As you think it repeatedly, you enlarge upon it, you add concepts to it, and you quietly and deeply think about love in its most abstract sense.

However, when I give a treatment for love, I relate it to either a situation, a condition or a person. If I am in a resentful state of mind, I treat myself to have a loving mental attitude. In treatment you synchronize your consciousness with the one mind, and give to that one mind a definite outlet into which it flows and by means of which it operates. I might treat for love in the relationships of a person. I might treat for love in the atmosphere of an office. I might treat for love in a family relationship. But it would be a specific thing which I treated.

You may need meditation, but I believe you certainly need treatment. When I wake up in the morning I may want to meditate on God, but if I should step out of the bathtub onto the tile floor and wrench my ankle, I then don't need meditation; I need treatment. I need to relate the power to a specific condition.

A treatment is nothing more or less than a directive action of the subconscious mind. The moment that will power enters in, it is no longer a spiritual treatment. It is then a human mind treatment, and a human mind treatment will do nothing but wear you out. If it creates any effect at all, it will be a temporary one. It will never be for the good of all or for the good of the individual.

In spiritual treatment, on the other hand, I realize that I am in a power which is already in action, and which I merely let happen through me. I clear my thought regarding a situation in order to let my good happen, because I am not treating conditions, I am treating consciousness. I am treating mental attitudes, moods, my thinking and feeling nature. I am doing this, knowing that back of my treatment, and in action through it, the creative mind is already thinking and the power is already acting. All I do is to let it out and give it direction.

Let me use this illustration: If you go to the faucet in your kitchen and turn it on, the water comes out. It doesn't come out until you turn it on; but its sole purpose is to come out, because water flows under a law of gravity. When you turn it off, it stops coming out, because a law makes it act that way.

Treatment is the mental process wherein you turn on the faucets of your mind and let power flow through. You do not have to force water out of the faucet; it comes. You do not have to pray for it to come out; it comes. You merely turn the faucet. The same thing is true of God. You do not ask God. You do not plead with God. You do not entreat God. You let God do it and the way in which you let God do it is by turning in thought to God and knowing that it is happening.

Start with the premise that the creative power of the infinite mind is already waiting to flow through you. Whenever you have a problem that needs treatment, at that point you have a blockage where life is not flowing. You have a shutoff of the eternal stream of power. Your treatment changes your consciousness from the negative to the positive. As it changes from the negative to the positive, the power flows through, because the power can only flow through a positive.

It is the nature of the creative power to take form, and it is the nature of man to direct it to the form he wants. You and I have every right in the world to use the power of God for our own use and for the benefit of other people. We have it, because we are it.

My treatment work is just as scientific, just as definite and just as complete in its action, as though I were using a book of recipes for cooking. I know that if I use ingredients correctly and cook them at the proper heat for the proper amount of time, I will have a result. When I direct my mind to the action of God, a knowledge of God, believing that it is now working through me, and that I have every right as its beloved creation to direct it, I give it a specific form through which to operate and I get a result. It's definitely a process and definitely a science.

Start on the basis that health, wealth, love and self-expression are yours by divine right, and that you have temporarily forgotten that they are yours. In your temporary spiritual amnesia, which is exactly what that is, you have believed that you did not have them. As the law of mind functions under a law of belief, your belief that you did not have them caused you not to have them.

By the same law, however, as you begin to believe that you have what you want, then you have it. It's one law acting two ways. This is the law of the soul, the law of the subconscious mind. You are a conscious thinker in a subconscious atmosphere. This is the essence of scientific treatment. Therefore, what you consciously think becomes a law to the subconscious to produce. What you clearly think takes form because it is the nature of the subconscious to project form. It doesn't do it because it wants to; like the water in the faucet, it does it because it has to do it.

Spiritually, you have always been healthy, only there have been lapses in your knowledge of this. You always have been prosperous, but there have been times when you didn't think you were. (Those are the moments I call spiritual amnesia.)

Start with the proposition of a perfect God, a perfect individual and a perfect world. You need a working knowledge of the nature of God, the nature of yourself as a spiritual being and the nature of your present universe as a spiritual activity. Heaven is right here and now, whether you know it in that language or not. Life is heaven or hell, according to your viewpoint of it. Your viewpoint of it is conditioned by your mental awareness of it. If you are in an unpleasant mood, you are in hell, and your world reacts to you as hell. If you are in a good mood, you are in heaven and your world reacts to you as heaven.

You start with the premise that God is perfect and God is all. Take as your secondary premise in treatment that you are the operation of this allness. If you are the operation of this allness, and if this allness is all, then your universe must be this allness. Say to yourself, "I am in the completeness and allness of God. I am that allness and completeness of God made visible. I exist in it, because it must be my world."

When I give a treatment, I make the above statement, because I want to be sure of my premise. God is perfect; spiritual man is already perfect; and this universe is now perfect. I merely condition my thought to perceive of it as that. That is why I insist that you should incorporate in your treatment a conscious recognition that the things you want you already have. If they always have been, then they are now, and always will be where you are.

If you have been ill and you are now well, you couldn't become well if you had not been well even when you were sick. You are the action of God, therefore you are the health of God. If you are always the health of God, the very fact that you became ill and then regained your health indicates that even when you were ill, you were healthy. You covered it up beautifully, for a short time. Health must have been in you or you couldn't have it again. If health is a spiritual idea operating in individual, then it is an eternal idea since God's ideas never stop. God's ideas never wear out and God's ideas are never limited to any one time, place or situation. They are the eternal function of the infinite spirit.

When you recover from an illness, you are returning to a mental conditioning which you previously had. Like the prodigal son, you have been away and wandered among the swine of bacteria, penicillin, sulpha and aspirin. After a while you weary of these and of their ideas and you return to what you have always been.

I begin my treatment with the understanding that I am not treating a sick person. I am treating a completely well person, because the well person was never sick. He or she was merely covered over with an incorrect belief in sickness.

The value of diagnosing a condition before you treat it is to know what to deny. When a person describes a condition to me, I immediately use strong denials:

It is not so, there is not a word of truth in it. It is an absolute lie. The only truth is that this individual is a perfect spiritual being, operating in a perfect body, living in a perfect world, because that is what God knows.

There is a value in admitting that you temporarily have an erroneous condition. You don't intend to keep on having it, but you have it temporarily, because you are temporarily believing it. You now stop believing in it and start believing in its opposite. As you stop believing the negative, by denying it out of your consciousness and start believing the positive by affirming it into your consciousness, then that which you deny disappears and that which you affirm appears again, because it has always been there. The energy and intelligence it takes to be sick is the same energy and intelligence which makes you well.

Here is an illustration. David Maxwell phoned me and said:

"I have a terrible cold and a very sore throat. I feel miserable. Will you give me a treatment?"

David told me three important things regarding his case. I made a list of what to deny. Taking the word cold, I treated against congestion. For sore throat, I treated for ease and comfort. For the word miserable, I treated for joy and happiness. I then gave the following treatment:

This treatment is for David Maxwell. I declare that there is only one presence, power, mind, law and action. All this is God, and all is operating in and through David. This being so, there cannot be a cold, for there is no emotional congestion to cause a cold. David is established in peace, harmony, order and right action. There cannot be a sore throat, because the throat is the physical symbol of the mental channel through which God's ideas are accepted by man. Therefore, I know that David is accepting the ideas of God and because they are the ideas of God, they flow into him and through him with ease, comfort and joy. They cannot make him ill. They can only make him perfect, easy and comfortable. God's ideas are always beneficent. They are always healing, blessing and benefiting man. There is no sore throat because God's idea are being received by David, with ease, comfort, joy and delight.

Then I add:

David Maxwell does not feel miserable, because man's feeling nature is the operation of love, God's love. Since it is the action of love, he cannot be miserable. This action produces expansion and delight. Therefore, David is now a perfect being in a perfect world, governed by a perfect God. Amen.

That is the way you give a treatment. Make a list of the negatives and go to work on them. Use a strong denial of each negative, when and as it appears. Don't wait until later.

As you read this book, learn to watch your thought and discipline your consciousness. Whenever you hear people speak negatives, say to yourself, "That is not so. I don't believe it and I won't accept it."

Deny evil as and when it happens. Silently within your own mind, constantly deny the negative and constantly affirm the positive. It is a twenty-four hour a day job that you have selected. But it is the only way you can treat yourself to happiness.

Treatment is the science of inducing within a mind a concept, not a thing. When you are aware of a need you usually interpret that need in terms of a thing, condition, situation or person. Realize that you never need a person, place or thing. You need an idea, a concept. Learn that the entire action of the universe is a mental action. Your point in this operative field of mind is that of a thinker, a perceiver of concepts, a perceiver of ideas. Whatever concept you accept, whatever ideas you accept, these will determine your experience in the world. Your goal in treatment is the correct perception of ideas. When you have an incorrect perception of ideas, treat yourself and induce within your mind proper concepts.

When you have something you don't want, you have it because you have a subconscious pattern of what you don't want. By denying the pattern of what you don't want, and affirming the concept of what you do want, you induce in your area of consciousness a conviction and a belief of what you do want, and the law of the subconscious takes it and produces what you want. Transfer your observation from the condition that you do not want to the condition that you do want.

When you put these principles into practice, the difference between you and your friends who do not know them is that when a problem arises you treat first and act secondly. The tendency of your friends is to start with a material remedy of some kind. For example, in your home you hurt yourself in some way. Having learned treatment, you immediately deny the condition and affirm the opposite. You establish your mind in order, and then you take the logical material steps. Your friends who do not know treatment act the opposite way. When they hurt themselves, they rush to the phone and call the doctor. Later they may say: "I should have prayed."

Think back a few days to a time when something negative happened. What was your first reaction? If your first reaction was to handle thought and you immediately denied the negative and affirmed the positive, you are learning how to treat.

You are in heaven to the extent that you are able to control your own consciousness. You do not experience heaven through a church, a religion or a book. You produce it through the disciplining of your own consciousness. You have heaven when you relax and realize that this world is a grand place. This world is a great adventure when you are feeling well, have enough money, are happy and have friends. That is why everyone takes a two weeks' vacation to experience heaven. On your vacation you have peace, joy and plenty. For two weeks you don't worry about anything, because you are enjoying yourself, and that is heaven.

This world is heaven, but you are not seeing heaven, and because you are not seeing heaven you are not experiencing it. You see heaven by clearing your own vision, not by changing the world. You see heaven by treating yourself to life, here and now.

2

Treat Yourself to Wealth

MONEY IS WONDERFUL! One day I told a man this and he had the usual reaction of rejecting my suggestion. Ned Robertson sat in my office and told me frankly he did not want any spiritual help.

"I have come only to please my wife," he said. "And the sooner I can get out of your office the more pleased I will be." He was ill at ease, nervous, and to me as the observer, he was a tragic figure.

Let me tell you about Ned. He fitted the pattern of the hard driving American business man. He had worked his way through college. He was then forced to take a mediocre office job, since he had to earn money to support his widowed mother. A few years later he married an ambitious wife. As each of his three children was born his financial pressures increased. The usual family illnesses, the death of his mother and the question of whether the children, who were now ready for college could or could not go, had brought him to my office.

"What is the one thing you have always wanted to do?" was the first question I threw at him.

19

It took ten minutes of conversation to make him take an honest look back through the years. Finally he said: "I've always wanted to be a sports fisherman."

"Well, why not do what you want to do?" I asked. "The universal will answer any demand made upon it. You can make money and be healthy only when you are doing what you want to do. You may make money doing what you don't want to do, but you lose out somewhere along the line."

"Man, I'm forty-five years old and in debt up to my ears, and you talk about my doing what I want to do?"

Three years later Ned Robertson was earning $95,000 a year as owner of a fleet of fishing boats in a Florida Keys resort. He was happy and in better health than he had ever known. His oldest son was in his third year of college, and his two other children were ready to enter.

I'll never forget his final remark as he left my office that first grim day:

"Your whole idea is preposterous, but I know you are sincere. I also know that you have helped many people to greater prosperity. What you've just told me is the craziest thing I've ever heard, but people tell me you've got something. I will come back next week and try it."

As the door closed, I knew that Ned was on the road to solving his problem. Gradually he learned to see that life is not a struggle, but that it is a cooperative process. After six sessions he was even willing to believe that a creative power could act through him, and would do so as he gave it direction. He started attending my church, and actually enjoyed it and profited by it. As his inner tensions were replaced by confidence that his own creative power was a spiritual potential present in everyone, he planned how to get out of his humdrum work and into the sporting life he loved.

The moment Ned Robertson changed from the man who knew what he could not do, into the man planning to do what he wanted to do, and knowing that he could do it, his demonstration began to appear. That same key is in your hands. Cease the endless contemplation of where you are and start contemplating where you want to go. It will work every time. It is the ancient teaching of every religion, and it is a demonstrable method.

Ned erased the pattern of poverty in his subconscious mind and replaced it with the pattern of prosperity. He realized that the money problem was in his thinking, and not his situation. He came to the subconscious conviction that God did not create him to live under the tension of financial difficulties. He erased the pattern of lack out of himself, once and for all, through daily treatment.

You can do the same thing. If you have a poverty pattern and you are unwilling to do anything about it, all right; then adjust to it and live that way, but don't complain. Relax and adjust. But if you want to do something about it, begin treating yourself today. You don't treat your sources of income. You treat only yourself.

If through some miracle, the government gave everyone in the nation $1000 a week, they would still be wanting more. Money is not the answer. The answer is never subsidy. The answer is the creative power which can be awakened in anyone who wants to find it, because God's mind is everywhere evenly present. Since God's mind is everywhere evenly present, it is in you and it is in you as a potential. It is in you as an intelligence which you can release and thereby change your world.

You do this by thinking prosperity. Prosperity is a pattern; it is a habit. Lack is a habit with most people. If lack is your habit, you are going to break that habit. Here you come up against the fact that a habit is hard to break. If you don't think so, ask the person who is a heavy smoker to stop. He will smoke even when he doesn't want to, because the habit pattern is there.

My own private, personal definition of a habit pattern is this: A habit pattern is a spontaneous action repeated by an individual until it becomes automatic. It is a pattern which starts in the conscious mind and then becomes subconscious. It is repeated often enough to become a pattern in the subconscious, and being a pattern in the subconscious, it will function there until it is nullified by another repeated action of conscious mind.

In other words, your present money consciousness will remain just about the same as it is now until you change the pattern. Fortunately there is within you the ability to change the pattern. You can do this without resorting to lengthy psychological therapy. You can change your pattern through a new understanding of God. In order to understand God, you have to understand the operation of your own thought. You change your money pattern by watching your conscious mind, seeing to it that it injects into your subconscious a new concept of abundance.

Your conscious and deliberate thought in larger terms goes into the subconscious upon repetition, and becomes a habit pattern. Your old limited pattern is destroyed and your new expanded pattern is established. Though this takes place automatically in the subconscious, it must be deliberately thought by the conscious. You can decide right now to think of God as abundance, to think in terms of prosperity. When you attain a pattern in your subconscious of such abundance, you will never lack again. You will never be limited again.

If you will constantly keep prosperity uppermost in your conscious mind, it will become a pattern, and when it becomes a pattern you will demonstrate it.

One of the great English teachers of treatment, F. L. Rawson, once told a congregation he was addressing that when he began his ministry he was in need of money. Not having enough money, he decided he would treat fifteen minutes a day for one year solely for money, ease, comfort and prosperity. Within a few weeks his whole financial condition changed. He never had to worry about money any more. He maintained the treatments, however, for one year. He told his students, "I will never again lack in my life. I have erased lack out of my mind once and for all. It will never again happen to me." Regardless of war or depression, it never did happen to him again, because he had destroyed the lack pattern out of his mind. He had replaced it with a prosperity pattern in consciousness.

Check your own thought right now. How much are you worrying about next year? Are you still worrying about a loss of money a year ago? Treat yourself today, saying, "Within me there are plenty of talents. I now change my consciousness from one of poverty to one of prosperity."

I define prosperity as the ability to do what you want to do at the instant you want to do it.

Money in the bank is a good idea. A few stocks and bonds tucked away are a good idea, and an intelligent life insurance program is wise. Why don't I define prosperity in terms of money? Because prosperity isn't money. Money is necessary for prosperity, and prosperity will produce it, but prosperity is not money.

If you are able today to do everything you want to do today, and can do it in the way you want to do it, you are prosperous. You are as rich as anyone with ten billion dollars. I learned years ago that I could demonstrate prosperity without a large reserve of money, because prosperity is the freedom to do what I want to do now, not in the future or in the past but now. If you can buy a good dinner today and later go to the theater, if that is what you want to do, you are as rich as Croesus. That is all you need for now, and that is prosperity. The diamond necklace you have wanted all your life, the yacht or the mink coat you can have, too, and I'll tell you about that. If you really want a diamond necklace you can have it. But, before you buy a diamond necklace find out what the insurance rates are on it; it's the upkeep that counts.

It is easier to demonstrate a diamond necklace than it is to demonstrate a spiritual state of consciousness. I had a friend who told me that years ago she had heard a lecture in which the speaker told his audience to visualize anything they wanted and they would demonstrate it. She and her friends had chuckled over this. One day she said to her sister:

"I'm going to demonstrate a diamond necklace." She did. She demonstrated quite a few other diamonds also, but the only trouble was that a disagreeable husband came with them. She made her demonstrations but it was not easy to handle the responsibilities which came with them.

Prosperity is the ability to do what you want to do at the instant you want to do it. You say, "But doesn't money still come into the picture?" What is this money we are discussing? Let's clear our thought on money by first looking at the universe. Authorities in the scientific field have made us realize that the universe is a fluidic creation; it is an eternally flexible creation. It is always in a state of flux. It never stops or stands still for an instant. It is energy forever expanding itself. It is intelligence forever finding new outlets for its own creative action.

As you view this universe of infinity, eternity and activity, and consider the planet of earth in relation to this great cosmic order, you behold a universal field of right action. The first necessity for understanding the world in which you live is to understand it on the premise that it is activity. It is never static. See yourself in a fluidic universe, a flexible universe that is forever in process of change. At the same time it is forever dominated and guided by an intelligence which is forever producing new forms, new creations, new experiences. All of these when seen rightly are good.

If you realize this you will then deal with your universe as a flowing thing. You will deal with your prosperity as a flowing action. The average person has stopped his own prosperity because he has concluded that prosperity is money in the bank, or money in investments, instead of seeing prosperity as an inlet or an outlet of activity.

There is a universal pulse-beat. This pulsating universe has its own measurements of stars and atoms. As an individual you have your own pulse-beat which denotes to the doctor the tempo of your circulatory system. But, remember that it is a circulatory system. It is an eternal activity taking place in you. In a well person this circulation is in balance, always in right relationship. When your pulse is taken, no matter whether it is fast, slow or average, it is the tempo of your circulation. Likewise there is a barometer for our national pulse-beat in economics. Many people pick up their evening newspapers, and the first news they read is the stock market page, the barometer or the pulse-beat of the financial day as it has been recorded. If the market goes down, they weep. If it goes up, they rejoice. They have become dependent upon a set of statistics presented to them by authorities in the financial field for their feeling of prosperity. The stock market is dependent upon buying and selling. It is a circulatory system, just as the pulse of your own body is dependent upon the beating of your heart, the circulatory system and the moving of the blood throughout your body. All life is circulation.

When you begin to fear lack, you should immediately begin to work on your own consciousness, not with the question of how you can make more money, but with the question:

"What do I need to have money circulating in my world?"

Prosperity is the circulation of money in your world. It is movement. It is activity. It is a flow. Poverty is the result of a misunderstanding of life. The universe is crammed with prosperity. The nation is rich in every-thing imaginable. You say you want riches, but how are you going to get them?

The older theologies have warned us that money is dangerous, that money is sinful. I do not believe that. There are, however, countless good people who do believe that. I look at them in amazement. While they believe that money is the root of all evil (Jesus did not say it was), at the same time they are always bothering their employers for a raise. I often think if you believe that money is evil, then why work for it? Why use it? Just go and live with some kind relatives and you won't need to bother about it.

I believe in prosperity, because I believe that prosperity is the action of God. I teach prosperity because I believe that it is the natural state of anyone who is willing to think in larger terms. A former teacher of mine says, "God loves a prosperous individual." It is my conviction that this is so.

Why does God love a prosperous man? Because the average prosperous person is less cluttered in mind than the person who worries about his finances. I have often said to people that there is seldom anything wrong with them which $1,000,000 or its equivalent wouldn't cure. The next time you have a state of depression, fear and worry, you may probably agree with me that there is nothing wrong with you which an upswing in business, an increase in income or an inheritance from an uncle couldn't cure.

Ninety per cent of the people who come to my office could be healed in two days by receiving $1,000,000. The sick would recover because they stopped worrying about money. The poor would be prospered temporarily. They would have their bills paid. The unhappy would all go on a vacation the next week and would be joyous again. You may say, "But what about the people who have a great deal of money? Will $1,000,000 make them happier?" I never knew a millionaire yet who couldn't use another million. I believe in prosperity as a spiritual system because it frees you for other things. That is the only value in it.

People say to me: "I don't understand why you, a spiritual teacher, believing in all that God is, carry life insurance."

My answer is that I carry life insurance so I don't have to worry about the future. That part of my life is taken care of. It takes that much pressure off my daily thinking and I can devote the greater part of my mind to my work and do it better.

That is why you should have prosperity. It gives you greater ease to do so many things. It takes away worry, limitations, those cords that bind, and it is definitely a spiritual idea. The universal spirit can work more easily through the creative, dynamic, positive mind of a prosperous individual. You are more positive, more creative and more dynamic, when you have a sense of security in money. When you feel prosperous you have an open mind in which new ideas can operate. That is why God loves a prosperous man.

The moment you realize this and shift your attention from the concept that money is evil, to the belief that money is wonderful, you begin to have a greater circulation of money in your life. Anything you love increases and anything you criticize moves out of your life.

The first step toward prosperity, as Ned Robertson learned in our work together, is to love money. Why? Because it is the means which God is using at the present instant to maintain a circulation in your world of economics. There must be circulation. Therefore, watch your damming it up, hemming it in or putting a fence around it, because the joker is still in that deck of cards. If you die one of these days, your relatives will have a free-for-all with it. That is the joker for people who hoard money.

Circulation is necessary to your body if you are to keep alive. Circulation is necessary to the general field of economics, if we are to have a healthy financial structure in the world. Circulation is necessary in your bank account or pocketbook, and even more than that in your mental attitude about money. You must believe that you are in a universe which is self-sustaining. If you are in a universe which is self-sustaining, then you must be a part of it and the creative process which causes the universe to be self-sustaining must likewise be in your affairs and cause your affairs to be self-sustaining.

The universe says that if you are wise in your use of money, if you are receptive to the idea of money, you will have money. No good thing is withheld from those who love God. Money is good, but you have to believe that money is good. Correct your thought about money.

Next, you must be willing to live in a state of financial flux, to live in a state of financial flexibility and meet it without fear. Do this and you will have more money. If only there were doctors of money, as there are doctors of bodies and doctors of the mind, life would be easier.

When the barometer on your bank account goes down, it is merely an indication that it will go up again; if you remain open to the idea of money. It is a common thing in the economic life of a nation to see men make great sums of money, lose great sums of money and ten years later again make great sums of money. These men have a healthy pattern of money. Their subconscious minds are saturated with the belief in ease, comfort, and money. They are willing to do the work to get it, and they expect it, so they have it.

Sell yourself on money as a spiritual idea until it becomes an automatic subconscious pattern in you. You can establish a subconscious pattern of prosperity through treatment as easily as you have previously established a subconscious pattern of lack. It is very easy to slip into a fear state on money. Such fear comes in subtly and quietly through the backdoors of your mind. "I'd better be careful. I'd better tighten up. I'd better withdraw. I'd better hold back. I'd better take it easy for a while."

So you withdraw, hold back, tighten and become tense. Things don't go right. You are tired. No matter how much sleep you have, you awake exhausted. All of a sudden you realize the vicious fear which you have allowed to creep in the backdoors of your mind. You have permitted the world to tell you what to do. You have allowed newspaper reports to influence you. You have allowed friends at dinner parties to advise you, instead of saying in your own mind:

As far as I know, this universe is a spiritual system, an accurate system. The universe responds to me as I respond to it. There is plenty of everything. I know in my subconscious mind that this is true, and it now happens. It can't happen if I let fear control me. It can't happen if I let people convince me of lack. It can only happen when my subconscious pattern of money is definite.

Know that money is not evil. Don't fear it. Don't condemn it. Merely use it.

I do not fear the lamp on the desk where I am writing. I merely use it. I am not afraid of it. I do not condemn it. It's a good lamp and it serves me well. Take the same attitude about money. Use it with intelligence. Use it as a symbol of the prosperity of God, and you will always have it. Live with money freely, easily and naturally. You are in the midst of a spiritual system which on every hand creates forms and shapes of abundance. The seed produces many plants. Everything starts as a seed-idea and becomes an abundance form.

The people who have the greatest freedom in money are those who no longer have to think about money. They have arrived at a subconscious conviction that they will always have it. Those who do have trouble getting money have not yet convinced themselves that they can live in this world and have the freedom and use of money. I do not mean millions of dollars. I mean enough to live more than comfortably.

You may ask—"But doesn't money come from work?"

The answer is, "No." There are business executives who work only two hours a day, or one day a week, and take a six weeks vacation whenever they desire, yet receive enormous salaries. They receive their money because they are considered to be worth that much money. The reason they are considered to be worth that much money is that they have convinced themselves that they are worth it. When you are convinced that you are worth more money, walk in to your employer and say you want a raise, and you will receive it. You will never get a raise, however, if you merely want a raise and are not convinced that you are doing a better job than you did a year ago. You will get your raise only when you are convinced in your own subconscious that you are worth it. You must first convince your own mind, for money is a subconscious conviction on your part. Accept the idea of money and say:

Money is God's idea of circulation. I now subconsciously accept
the idea of money. I accept this divine idea without limitation.
I do not think of money in terms of any amount. I think of it
in terms of plenty to maintain me in ease and freedom of action.

Don't treat in terms of amounts because wealth is a
relative thing. The universal mind always gives plenty
and to spare. I am weary of having just enough to meet
my current bills. I want a little to spare.

Spending money is wonderful if you spend it with intelligence. There should always be a portion of your
money which you spend to have real fun. I don't mean
polite fun. Polite fun is doing what someone else thinks
is fun. I'm talking about real fun. Whatever is the thing
that brings joy to your soul you should do, whether anyone else likes it or not.

Every year of my life I ride on a roller coaster, and I
intend to continue to do that. It's one of my ideas of fun.
I don't want to do it every day, I don't want to do it even
once a week, but I do want to do it occasionally. Ministers shouldn't ride on roller coasters, and congregations
shouldn't see ministers riding on roller coasters. Anyone
in my position ought to have more dignity than to ride
on a roller coaster, but I still occasionally ride on a roller
coaster. Be normal, be free, accept abundance and use it
in an intelligent, normal way. Use it in a way that gives
you freedom to have a creative release of life.

The universal supply expresses through a law of abundance without a secondary law of limitation. You may
treat for abundance with an unconscious pattern of limitation. So you do not have results. On the surface you
say that you desire plenty of money, but your subconscious pattern is $325 a week. As the subconscious pattern

has more power than the temporary conscious mind desire, you demonstrate $325 a week while you could be demonstrating much more. The universe takes you at your valuation. Increase the consciousness of your own valuation in money. As you do this more money appears in your experience.

All treatment is an action of the conscious on the subconscious. Treat yourself to prosperity this way:

> *I like money. I believe that it is God's activity, that it is good. I use it with wisdom. I release it with joy. I send it forth without fear, for I know that under a divine law it comes back to me increased and multiplied.*

If you will use the above treatment daily and subconsciously accept it, you will be amazed at the results.

Money is a spiritual activity. It is good. It is wonderful and we should love it. It is not filthy lucre, it is not sinful, it is not the devil's playmate. It is God in action. The stock market is a financial barometer. I do not condemn it. I do not criticize it, nor do I bless it. I use it as an orderly part of my business world. I do not worry about the value of dollars, because whether values go up or down, I am convinced within myself that I am worth money and will always have it. I will always have money, because the law of prosperity is based on the perpetual circulation of God's ideas in the infinite mind.

A great circulation of creative thought is pouring into your consciousness now and appearing in your world as cash. This process goes on eternally despite the value of a dollar or the value of a pound sterling. If you believe that your money is dependent upon the stock market or that your money is dependent upon valuation, or that your money is dependent upon hours of work, you are living under bondage. You do not demonstrate money. You demonstrate more worry, more watching, more fear, because that is where you have placed your attention. You are setting up cause, so you reap a similar effect, since cause and effect are one.

Your entire thinking is the creative power in your world. If you worry about money then the effect must be like unto the cause and you only have more worry about less money. This is completely logical as well as completely true. It is necessary to take your attention from money as a necessity of life, and think of it as a God-given idea. It is the normal circulatory system of the present age.

I want to close this chapter with a specific mental treatment for money. I want you to be clear on this idea. I am not giving you a treatment to increase your salary. You are treating for money. Read and declare audibly this treatment. Be willing to take any form of money when it comes. If someone stops you on the street and invites you to a dinner, accept. Let your money come from any direction. I have known people who gave themselves a money treatment. Immediately afterwards a friend would say to them:

"May I take you to lunch?" And they would answer, "I couldn't accept."

If someone says to you, "I want to give you something" and it is at all usable, take it. If it isn't usable, take it anyway and give it to someone else, because that is the way card party prizes circulate.

Remember that money is God in action. It is a spiritual idea in your life. You should welcome with joy anything resembling it. Be a little enthusiastic about money. Don't criticize anyone who has it. If you believe that someone is receiving money dishonestly, what of it? He is working under the law of his own negative mind and he will be stopped. Don't worry about it. It is none of your business, and don't criticize him. Think of money as being God in action, and whenever you see large amounts of money, say to yourself, "Isn't that wonderful!"

This human mind of ours has its tricks of limitation and it gives itself away every time. If you treat yourself for prosperity and then criticize someone else because he has plenty of money, it doesn't make sense, does it? The mental work you have done is rendered ineffective, because your own criticism of money has erased its value.

You are going to like money because it is God in action. You are going to use it with wisdom, release it in joy and know it will return to you increased. Say to yourself:

I always have had enough money to meet my needs and the infinite spirit will never stop my income. There is no blockage in the universal system; the universe is always in a state of flux. If there is a block in the flow of money in my life, it must be a temporary human block which I have within my own consciousness. I now break that block. I accept money, appreciate money, use money and shall never again be afraid of not having money.

Treatment for Prosperity

I now subconsciously accept this treatment. There is only one creative cause, God. There is only one mind, God. There is only one life, God. There is only one substance, God. This present universe is the glory of God. It is a moving, flexible, fluidic creation. It is alive with life, the abundance, and the richness of God. I abide in prosperity. Mind created me in order that it might act through me. Therefore, I am receptive to its abundance. I am receptive to its circulation in my life in the form of money. Money is God's idea of circulation in my world of finance. I accept this idea completely. I appreciate this idea; I like it. Money being God in action is absolute good, it is wholesome. It is a blessing to me, and I am now prospered with it. I have no fear of lack for I believe that I have plenty of money. It is God's activity in my world. It is God's activity in my bank account, it is God's activity in my investments. It is God's activity in everything to which I lay my hands. This money is flowing, this money is free. I do not attempt to lock it up, I do not put a fence around it. It is God's money. I let it flow in, I let it flow out. As I release it, I know that it comes back to me, pressed down, shaken together and running over. "The Lord is my shepherd, I shall not want." I am now free in money. I rejoice in it. I appreciate it, and I thank God for it. I have money forevermore. Amen.

3

⌒⌒

Treat Yourself to Love

WE HAVE PRODUCED a generation of unhappy people. The last one hundred years have given us greater comforts and greater ease than have been known in the history of the world. At the same time, however, they have produced more frustration and incompleteness.

People look upon the word love either as a religious term or one dealing with sex. They fail to realize that their whole yearning for a full and rich life is the inner impulsion of love seeking a release through them as its logical outlet.

I am writing of love as the essential expression of whole living. Other books will tell you how to meet the right man or the right woman. This one is not written for that purpose. Life is either integration, disintegration or a mixture of both. Your happiness is in direct ratio to your ability to give yourself to others. Not all can do this easily, and some not at all, without extensive subconscious changes.

Remember, that you can always change the patterns in your subconscious through treatment. Don't let anyone convince you that you cannot, or that it takes years to do so. I have seen hundreds of people change from cold, hurt, "chip on the shoulder" personalities into gracious, outgoing expressions of life. Some have done this through psychological therapy, others through religion, and today thousands are realizing, through treatment, that the essence of life is cooperative action.

No man lives unto himself alone, and you will err if you try to do it. Lonely people are a drug on today's market. You can be lonely in a big family as easily as alone in a one-room apartment. A lonely person is a lonely person anywhere. An unhappy person is an unhappy person anywhere. Like any other negative habitual state of consciousness, basic pattern, or mental attitude, loneliness is a serious thing. It is not always self-induced, but it is at least self-maintained. Something can be done about it. I think that most lonely people have always been lonely, though they will say to me:

"Until now I have never been lonely."

I have studied the human mind long enough not to believe that. Loneliness probably was always an incipient pattern in that person. A recent series of events brought it to the surface and gave it added vitality, but it was always in the subconscious as a basic habit pattern.

It's a wonder that we aren't all more lonely than we are. As a child you were always lonely. Think back to your own childhood with honesty, taking away the lace and the froth, without blaming your parents or your environment. Look at your childhood with an open mind, and see if in your own experience your childhood wasn't very lonely. Not that your father and mother didn't love you—that had nothing to do with it. Your parents, no matter how much they loved you, were incapable of operating at your child level. Nor were you neglected. Your mother and father didn't make you lonely intentionally. Most adult minds are unable to understand the operation of the child mind and to know how to feed the emotional needs of a child. Even if you had eight brothers and four sisters, if you will be honest, you will probably find that those first five or ten years were lonely ones. This loneliness pattern comes to the surface of your mind at times throughout your life.

You can remember many times when you were desolate with loneliness. You were lonely and you were unhappy and you probably wept. Some people are naturally able to make an adjustment. They move into a cycle in which they are surrounded by friends; they mingle with ease and go through life with many loved ones and friends.

Such was the story of a woman who came to see me. When she was sixty-four, her husband died. The emotional shock threw her back to a childhood pattern which had remained dormant in her subconscious mind. Her years of married life had kept it covered, but had not cured it. This woman did not want to and certainly did not mean to, but she repeated her pattern of loneliness. She became bitter. I have never known a lonely person who wasn't at the same time a bitter person. Even if you think you know someone who is lonely and not bitter, on closer study you will find them bitter on some subject.

If you are a lonely person there is something you can do about it. Loneliness is never created of your own free will, it grows on you gradually. It comes from a series of minor hurts, little disturbances and very shortly it has you in its grasp.

Another woman came to my office last year who pro-
tested too much. She told too many people how much
she loved to live alone, how glad she was to have her
lovely little room in which to live quietly. Actually, she
was desperately unhappy. She confided in me, "I am
lonely, but I refuse to admit it, so I tell everyone that I
love it." But she didn't. Nobody wants to be alone, because it is unnatural. Lonely people develop peculiar
traits.

Whether you are seeking friendship, happiness or
marriage, treatment will help you to annihilate your
loneliness once and for all. First, clarify your own mind
by realizing that God is an infinite intelligence and an
infinite love and that right now both of these qualities
are operating for you. In your affairs, intelligence and
love are at work. When these two qualities working together operate in and through you with your consent,
you will find the problem of lack of love or loneliness
met. I can hear you ask, "How do I do it?"

There is a statement I have used for a number of years.
I started using this statement at a time in my life when I
was lonesome, and it worked for me. A positive spiritual
statement works for you. It sets up a new activity in consciousness which produces a new experience in your life.
The statement is this:

*Divine love brings together and maintains together those who
belong together, that the Glory of God shall be made manifest.*

When I use the word love in a spiritual sense, I am not
speaking of sentimentality. I like sentimentality. I enjoy

it; but when I use the word love, I am dealing rather with what I feel is the cohesive action of the universe. Love is the power which draws ideas together and maintains them in right relationship. In the material world, it maintains atomic structures in unity. The reason this book doesn't fall apart and become a heap of atoms on the floor is because there is a law of cohesion in operation. The cohesive action of the material world, whether maintaining a book or a car, is merely the out-picturing of the cohesive action of order. This same cohesive law draws together people who are alike.

One person said to me, "I never bring anyone new into my life, no matter how much I treat, except those who are just as lonely as I am. They haven't anywhere to go either."

I explain that the law of love, this cohesive law, can draw together only that which is similar. It cannot draw together that which is in opposition. The finest chef never has made oil and vinegar blend completely for a salad. You have tried to do this by shaking the dressing and hoping it would get on the salad before it separated again. Oil and vinegar will not blend together because there is no cohesive action between the two. Nor can you take lonely people and surround them with happy, friendly, extroverted people and expect them to mingle, because you have two different types of consciousness.

In mind, ideas group together under a cohesive law much as things do in the material world. Therefore if you who are lonely are to become less lonely you have to begin at the point of cause. The point of cause is an unconscious pattern of which you are unaware. You certainly did not induce loneliness intentionally, but nevertheless it is there.

If you are alone and unhappy say to yourself:

There is a pattern in my subconscious mind which is causing this condition. I now erase it. I now put in my mind a pattern of companionship. I realize that in the mind of God which created perfect people there could not be lonely, unhappy individuals, for God made us to be one. Therefore in my individual life, there cannot be a pattern of loneliness. I am created by the mind of this universe to live in association with people, with love, warmth, friendship and a spontaneity of joy. I now believe that this is mine. I now project love to my fellow man.

Examine the lives of most lonely people and you will find that they have nothing to give to their world but the past. They rarely discuss a current novel or a current news item. Always they discuss the joys and sorrows of the past. If you are one of these people, you should change your pattern. Try to talk about something new, fresh and different. Of course if you haven't read a new book, you can't do that. If you haven't been to a new play on Broadway or a new movie in your home town, you can't discuss it. Do something new, and you have a new topic of conversation.

Realize in your mind that God never made a lonely person. The pattern of loneliness can be broken if you really want to break it. It can be broken if you will use a spiritual technique with which to break it. Declare that love is in circulation in your life and that this love is flowing to you, through you and from you to your fellowman. Where you walk the flowers of hope spring up. Wherever you go you release a presence of joy, interest and alertness. Then people look across the room at you and think, "I'd like to talk to that person. She looks as though she has something interesting to say."

You cannot learn to treat unless you learn to love. No person can treat in an unloving state of mind. An effective treatment will transform you into a loving person. If you are greatly disturbed, unhappy and bitter, you had better start your treatment with definite statements of love, order and peace of mind. Treat against resentment, saying, "There is no resentment, for God in me is perfect understanding of my fellowman."

When you begin your regular daily treatment, be sure that you have a consciousness of love. If you try to do it while you are in a negative, unpleasant mental attitude, you will get no results, and you will have wasted your time.

If you have only ten minutes to treat and you are not in a good mood, then take nine and one-half minutes treating your consciousness for love and take the last half minute on your problem. It is your state of consciousness, not the language or the vocabulary, which determines the efficacy of the treatment. The atmosphere of successful treatment is love. By this I mean intelligent self-expression and a sense of being one with everything. Love is that quality which makes you feel you are one with your universe. When you say you love your husband, wife, mother, son, or daughter, you mean that in almost all of your basic patterns you are pretty much one with them. Not that you think alike, because that means regimentation. But your responses to life are pretty much alike.

You love people who respond to life as you respond to it. You want people around you whose general reac-

tions are like yours. Love is the feeling that you are one
with someone or a group. You don't have to agree with
everything that the other says or does. You are one in
the basic issues of life. In this oneness you leave the other
person free to develop as he so desires. If you love, you
must love enough to let the other person make mistakes.
There is an order in the universe. There is law, and then
there is love. When you love, you let everyone use the
law of mind in his own way.

You are going to make love the center of your life. To
be more loving, however, you have to be more wise, more
orderly and more law abiding. A great many people who
think they are loving are really just foolish people. They
make a four-star production of loving everyone, thereby
getting themselves into some very difficult situations, because they express love without wisdom.

You know children who are loved but not disciplined.
They are the terrors of the neighborhood. They are the
bane of existence to school teachers, and even their Sunday School teachers would like to spank them occasionally. Their mothers love them, their fathers love them,
everyone loves them, but no one has ever given them a
sense of order.

Your first concept of God should be order, and your
second concept should be love. Otherwise you will have
love without order. The law of cause and effect operates
whether or not you like it or believe in it. Since you are
living in this universe of order, it will respond to you as
you respond to it.

Love without order is confusion; love without order is
practically neurosis. You can only love intelligently and
with wisdom after you have established order and are
willing to accept the responsibility of living in a universe

that is governed by law. Only then are you in a position to learn how to get along with other people, to have friends, to release the love which is in you.

You were born to get along with people, to be friendly and loving. It is your automatic nature to express love and to receive it. You and I, in reality, are not separate and distinct people. We are all parts, one of another; we are all branches, one of another; we are all variations, one of another.

While you appear to be a distinct individual, yet that distinction as an individual is only your capacity of awareness. At the basis of God's consciousness we are all one in the subconscious. Individuality and personality are functions of the conscious mind only.

Every person in your world is actually a part of yourself. Every individual that is now, ever has been, or ever will be, must exist at this instant somewhere. Because he exists at this instant somewhere, he must be a part of your consciousness, because we are all one in the subconscious. Therefore, when you disagree with anyone, you are disagreeing with part of yourself. When you love someone, you are loving a phase of your own being. We are all one in spirit. We are all one in God. We are all expressing a unity in diversity.

Since there is a unity which operates as a diversity among all of us, variety is necessary to the functioning of God. If variety is necessary to the functioning of God, then the individual in his conscious phase of mind is fulfilling this divine plan.

Give to the people of your world the freedom to be themselves. At the same time claim your own right to be yourself. There is a chance that you may get along together. People with whom I do not get along are those who are either attempting to reform me, or whom I am attempting to reform. In other words, I forget that they are unique, distinct individualizations of an all-knowing intelligence which will take good care of them if I will leave them alone.

I have seen more family situations healed by someone taking his hands off his relatives than I have ever seen by anyone forcing his ideas on his relatives. When you let go of a person and relax, divine intelligence will operate in the other person, but it can't operate as long as you are seeking to superimpose your ego on his. Whenever you attempt to reform anyone, you are attempting to reform him from the basis of your own human standards. It is not your self-appointed mission to reform anyone, especially the people with whom you live or work or the people with whom you attend church.

When anyone tells me that he loves everyone and anyone, he is either fooling himself, or he is a very spineless person. I don't think it is possible on this plane of life to agree completely with everyone all the time and still maintain your individuality, which you must maintain as a spiritual being. You are alive to be different. Through all these varieties, these differentiations, man is displaying to the universe the infinite variableness of spirit. The creative mind is a mind of infinite variableness, forever creating new concepts. You and I are all expressing life differently. It is only in our points of differentiation that we are valuable to God and to man.

Each of you is a different level of consciousness. That doesn't mean that you have to decide whether you are at a higher or lower level than the others in your world.

Egotists are certain always that they are at a higher level. Inferiority types are certain that they are on a lower level. Probably we are all at about the same level, with slight variations or slight gradations. God's divine uniqueness is spiritual variety functioning at different levels of consciousness. The person with whom you work, or with whom you talk, is living at a different level of consciousness than the one in which you are functioning. Knowing this, you have two different viewpoints. Though you may eat the same food, sit at the same desk, do the same things, read the same books and go to the same church, you will have different viewpoints. That is necessary and that is right.

When a wife tells me that she completely understands her husband, she doesn't know it, but she is not telling the truth. No woman completely understands any man, and no man certainly ever claims to understand a woman. If it were possible for me to understand you completely, then you would have lost your individuality. You would no longer have a divine essence that is yours alone; it would now be mine too. There are depths to your consciousness which even you have not completely fathomed, and no one completely understands himself. That is why anyone who is going to be a psychoanalyst must go through a complete psychoanalysis. With all of his medical knowledge, with all of his psychological studies, he is still not equipped to heal and to help until he has undergone the therapy himself.

The individual's unique traits were never intended to be lumped together so that he loses his individuality. The brotherhood of man, which is a spiritual ideal, and which we are seeking to make a concrete possibility, is a way of functioning in which each person remains an individual

of his own volition. Each does those things which are
creative and constructive, not only for himself but for all
other people in the groups of which he is a part. We
would have no difficulty in having this brotherhood of
man right here and right now, if each person were completely honest, decent and kind. Our problems do not
come from the masses. Our problems do come from
those individuals who take their own individuality, their
own uniqueness, their own peculiar gift from the heart
of God, and divert these to ends and purposes for their
own gain, thus destroying some good in the lives of other
people.

You will begin to get along with other people if you
first believe they all are born of a common cause—God.
By their nature they are supposed to be unique. It is not
up to you to change the uniqueness of any other living
soul on earth. Don't reform anyone; don't attempt to understand anyone completely. Don't attempt to dominate
anyone. Let God run His own world and let the infinite
spirit operate through each individual. If someone you
know does not want to let God operate through him, it
is none of your business. The most difficult thing to do
is to take your hands off another when you see him deliberately choosing to do evil. It is not up to you to be
his saviour.

Many of you know the writings of Kahlil Gibran, one
of the great spiritual thinkers of this age. Gibran, in his
most famous book, *The Prophet*, emphasizes individual
freedom in his chapters on love, friendship, marriage
and children. He states, "But let there be spaces in your
oneness."* He warns you that children are born through

* Page 19, *The Prophet* by Kahlil Gibran. Alfred A. Knopf, New York.

you, but not to you. Children are not born for the purpose of projecting the parents' ego. Rather they are a
means by which God expresses His individuality, and
parents should watch the unfoldment of their child's individuality and glory in it.

Don't force personal relationships. Let them happen.
You have never really selected a friend in your life.
Friendship happens; if people are not drawn to you by
right of your own state of consciousness, they will never
be friends. Let there be spaces between you and those
whom you love so that each may maintain his own unique
rights and gifts. The Spirit of God is in man, but the
Spirit of God is never one of uniformity. It is never one
of regimentation. Its automatic nature is to create variety, and in variety you abide and function.

What to do when you have an argument is a common
question. Jesus said that when you go to the altar to pray
and are angry with your brother, forgive yourself first.
He didn't say that you should go to your brother for
forgiveness, but to yourself. If he with whom you have
disagreed is really one with you in spirit, the condition
will right itself without explanation. If he is not, then let
him go, but clear your own thought about him. Be like
Jacob who wrestled all night with the angel, and said, "I
will not let thee go except thou bless me."

What another person believes is none of your business. Your only business is to be certain that you are
thinking rightly about your fellowman. Nor is it your
business what anyone thinks about you. Your only business is to think rightly about him.

You cannot run another person's mind. You have tried
to do that for years and have merely worn yourself out

in trying. When a person is active in your life, try to see him as he is. If he always makes a certain mistake, you shouldn't be annoyed. That is his pattern of behavior. That is his state of consciousness. That is the way he is. You can either take it or you can leave it. If you need this person in your world, then you might just as well adjust to his errors and not bother about them. Relax and when they happen, chuckle a bit and go on your way.

Many a marriage or business relationship has been wrecked because one of the partners couldn't put up with some minor persistent fault on the part of the other. If you have lived twenty years with a husband who has a bad habit, you should have changed the situation the first year, or at the end of twenty years you should be immune to it. But what happens at the end of twenty years? You finally explode!

If you are going to get along with people, you will find that you have to take them as they are and not attempt to change them. The annoyance which appears should be handled at the time it appears. If you don't like it, then move out of its influence, or move it out of your influence. Otherwise see it, handle it, and refuse to let it get under your skin.

If a man has lived with his wife for fifteen years and she still can't balance her checkbook, then either he should continue to live with her and balance her checkbook, or he shouldn't be surprised when she is unable to balance it. It would seem that after fifteen years, he would know what her pattern is and not be annoyed. If you like people, you can forgive them seventy times seventy. Yet, it is not a case of forgiving them; it is realizing that they will always react in certain ways. Cease attempting to reform them, and start informing yourself about them. On this basis, you can get along with anyone, because the person who you think is so difficult is actually a son of God, and it is your job to know this and to be wise in your dealings with him.

If you seek peace with your friends, you will find peace. If you are willing to work within yourself until you have changed your concept of them, then they will appear in your world in a different way, and your reaction to them will be changed. God in action through you loves and cooperates with every man.

I would like to close this chapter with a treatment for love:

The mood of the infinite mind is one of love. The action of intelligence takes place in loving ways. What God hath wrought has been by means of love. Knowing this, I realize that the love of God uses me as a center of its distribution. I let my mind be a center of God's intelligence. I let my heart be a center of His love. Living the life of truth is a warm and joyous experience. I let God's ideas rule my mind and I let God's love act through my heart.

There is nothing within me to impede the love of the spirit. I now release all personal opinions about others. I let go of all hurts and prejudices. I let the full action of Divine love act through me and be the basis of all human relationships. I am unified with the good in every man, and all else becomes as nothing. I have no interest in other people's faults. I keep my attention on the divine possibility within everyone I know. God's love is at the center of all, and it forever moves in perfect action through all. I am blessed and prospered by divine love. It enriches my soul and it prospers my consciousness. It frees me from mistakes of human judgement, and makes me to know that I am one with all good.

With love in my heart, I forgive and forget all untruth. The true spiritual man is all that I know of each person with whom I live, work and play. All else is unimportant, for God's love in me is interested only in the good, the true and the perfect. I think rightly, and I love greatly. This love flowing out from me is felt and recognized by others. In turn they love me and judge me according to God's standards. I love to let love express through me.*

* From *Richer Living* by Ernest Holmes and Raymond Charles Barker. Copyright 1953 by Ernest Holmes and Raymond Charles Barker.

4

∽

Treat Yourself to This Day

RUTH WELSH WALKED into my office one cold January day.
The very way she sat down indicated her hopelessness.
Her face was drawn and tired. Her first sentence was:

"My career is at a standstill, and I can't get a break, no
matter how hard I try."

I questioned her about her past. Instantly she came to
life and described her past successes with great vitality.
Her brown eyes became animated and bright. Her position in the chair changed to one of ease and authority.
She was at home in her past.

"What do you plan to do in the next five years?" was
my next query. Her vitality, animation and interest were
retained as she told of her hopes and visions of tomorrow. But when I asked her about her affairs of the moment, the old despair returned, the slouch and the strain
were again present.

Yesterday and tomorrow held Ruth in a vise-like grip.
Her full mental attention and emotional response were
channeled to the yesterdays and the tomorrows. She had
unconsciously become a victim of her own misuse of

mind. Gradually and carefully, I pointed this out to her. Following our talk and my treatment, she began to gear her mind to the present day, to the now, and new doors opened for her.

I personally believe in the immediate demonstration of God in your world. Unless you are experiencing a good right now, you cannot say that you are spiritually-minded. Every spiritual teacher who has ever appeared has lived in freedom in the midst of limitation. The Bible is filled with stories of men who did not wait for good to happen to them; they produced their own good out of themselves. These people, wherever they were, unconsciously realized that they were in their right place and that it was the right moment to create good. So they did it.

In most religious instruction there has been a delaying action. Followers of those religions expected results in life after death, rather than now. In treatment, however, you do not wait for results in life after death; you expect results here and you expect them now. This is perfectly logical, perfectly right and it is good.

At present you probably do not think of yourself often in spiritual terms. When you define yourself to yourself, you usually indulge in self-depreciation. When you think about yourself, you rarely think about your potentialities. In treatment you are supposed to do just that. You should think of yourself as the eternal potential of all that God is. You should think of yourself as the channel through which the mind of God acts.

There is one universal intelligence forever acting through a creative process. It always has been and it is now. It must be where you are at this instant, and it must be capable of producing whatever you direct it to do. Whatever the nature of the creator is, it must be omnipresent in its creation. It must act through its creation or otherwise it would not have created it. Divine intelligence has never created a useless object. It has never created a useless idea, and the intelligence which created man is the intelligence which acts through man. It is the intelligence which you are at this split second as you read this sentence.

If that is so, why doesn't your treatment always work immediately? Why don't you, reading this book, have an instantaneous healing, an immediate sense of great joy, enthusiasm, a feeling that everything is all right, and that every problem is solved? Because this infinite power, this unlimited mind, can only operate through you as you let it. The unlimited power is conditioned and limited by you, not by itself.

As soon as you can believe that all time is now and all place is here, your demonstration can happen now. It does happen like that every day for people who learn to treat. Suddenly they realize that they no longer have the problem they had when they started treating. A demonstration is a manifestation, a prayer answered. It is the thing accomplished which you desired to achieve. When your word takes form, it is a demonstration. When your desire is given a subconscious mold and becomes objectified in your life, it is a demonstration. You give thanks as you give your treatment because you know that supply and demand are one, and that your request is instantly manifested by the law of God.

How can you free yourself of the limitation of time, the delay, which you have placed on the action of God as it moves through you into form? First, use your own logic and reason. They will take you part of the way. Logic and reason tell you that if anyone can overcome difficulties, you can do the same. A law which works for one, works for all; otherwise it isn't a law. If the person working next to you in your office can be promoted, you can be promoted. If a person in your home can over-come a cold in three hours, you do not need to take three days to be rid of it. Reason and logic tell you that you are in the midst of a life process, which is the action of God, the action of intelligence, the action of law and order. These must be in action through you; and if they are in action through you, then you need not wait longer for your good. The only time necessary to produce a demonstration is the time it takes to clear your own thought.

You may ask, "Doesn't it take time to heal my body? Doesn't it take time to make changes in my business af-fairs?" These questions reveal your own conditioning in time. You are limited by your belief in time. Life re-sponds to you in the terms of your mind. Its response to you is not determined by the way it responds to anyone else. It is determined only by yourself. If you believe that it will take you a long time to do something, you accept that time allotment in your mind, and thus into your experience. The reason it will take so long a time is not that life takes that amount of time to produce what you want; it is that you have subconsciously decided it will take that long.

Most chronic invalids expect a long, slow recovery and that is what they get. People who have not been sick in many years have instantaneous healings more easily than do people conditioned to sickness. A chronic invalid lives

under the law of delay. Everyone tells him that he will
be better next week, next month or come Christmas. So
he continues being ill; a chronic invalid is an incipient
dictator who has gone to bed.

Your experience is determined by your consciousness.
God is not waiting; life is already in action. The thing
you want, you already have, but you do not know it. God
believes you have it. That statement sounds utterly in-
comprehensible, but it is the truth. Jesus lived in a world
which, if he had permitted it, would have conditioned
him in every way possible. He always had the health he
wanted, the money he needed. He did the things he
wanted to do. He wore good clothes, traveled with a fine
group of people, and he enjoyed eating at a rich man's
table.

Jesus was unconditioned by time. He stood in the midst
of a conditioned world, which said to him, "You can't."
And he replied, "Yes, I can. There is a power within me
that will do it." When people told him of limitations obvious in his experience and environment, he said calmly,
"All power is given unto me in heaven and in earth." He
refused to believe that time was a limiting factor. He
stood at a point in space, at an instant in time, and spoke
truth and demonstrated truth. I am sure his friends advised him to wait until King Herod died, because the
next king might be more friendly. Others advised him to
wait until the old high priest Caiaphas died, for the next
might be more tolerant. But Jesus did not wait. He could
easily have gone to a different country and taught a life-
time. There he could have lived as long as he wanted to,
and taught many thousands of people. He could have
trained great numbers of disciples, but he was a very wise
man. He knew that the time was now and the place was

where he was. He knew that if there ever was a heaven, he was already in it. "The Father is in me, and I in him," he said. Jesus knew that whatever the creative process was, it had to operate at that instant, not later.

There is an unconditioned action of God possible in you. It doesn't know that you are ill. It doesn't know that you are unhappy. It doesn't know that you are tired. It doesn't know that you had a difficult week. If you condition your mind with these negatives I have just mentioned, then you are conditioned by your own choice. If you want a difficult week ahead of you, you can have it; the Lord doesn't care. The infinite mind says, "Little man, make up your mind. Whatever you decide, that you will have." The infinite forever waits on the finite, and it forever creates through the finite what the finite decides it shall produce.

There is only one mind, the creative mind of this universe. There is only one law of its action, and it is acceptance and belief. You are in the midst of a power which is saying to you, "Use me, direct me, express me. I am ready. Are you?"

Mind at the human level hesitates, "In a few days or a few weeks, I'll be ready. I expect to have a good income two years from now. In twenty-five years I hope to have enough money to retire." The infinite process says, "All right, you have told me to delay, so I will." You could have your demonstration today, but you think you can't, so you won't.

Your conditioning determines your experience. How can you treat to be unconditioned by time and space? Declare that you are a spiritual being. Declare that as a spiritual being, a son of God, you must be in an unlimited, creative power. You cannot conceive of the power which created this universe as limited. Where you are, you are not limited, and you convince yourself of that in treatment. Having convinced yourself, you declare what you want. Never follow the old pattern of taking your burdens to the Lord in prayer. You always told God what you did not want, so you received more of it. You always receive what you declare, proving the power of the spoken word. If you try to take your burdens to the Lord, you will have more burdens. While it may be virtuous to be a martyr, it is spiritually unsound.

When you do your daily treatments, affirm the desires of your heart. Declare your highest vision of good, and that it is now so, not next year but right now.

You may say, "That is illogical." If you investigated the miracles of Jesus on the basis of logic, you would have to stop even before you started. Jesus could stand before a sick person and deny that there was a sick person. He didn't say, "O Lord, heal this sick woman." He said to the woman, "You are well," and she was. He didn't stand in front of five thousand hungry people and say, "O Lord, I hope the bread lasts. O Lord, feed all these hungry people." He gave thanks that there was more than enough bread, and there was.

That is what you do in treatment. You look at your problem frankly, but refuse to accept the problem, and instead accept the solution. You accept the demonstration now, not next year, not tomorrow, but now. When you accept it in that way, it happens in that instant.

I do not know what your problems are; I do know that the time is now, and the place is here. You don't need to finish reading this book, even this chapter, with your problems still attached to you. You arrive at the point where you say to your problem:

I no longer accept you. You have managed me long enough. I
refuse to accept you as a power in my experience for one more
second. Be gone. I now accept your opposite. I accept the health
of God. I accept the peace of God. I accept the unlimited money
of God. I am unconditioned by time and space. My good is
delivered to me now.

If you can do that, you will no longer experience your
problem. Guard your thought and hold to these ideas.
You will have results that you have never thought possible before. Treat yourself today and cancel your belief
in conditioned time, space, environment and heredity.
They are false conclusions of the human mind.

A demonstration doesn't depend on the length of your
treatment, the language you use or your condition at the
time you give it. It depends solely on your ability to clear
your thought regarding your condition.

A major reason some demonstrations come through
quickly and others take longer is that you and I know so
little about our subconscious, which is a conglomeration
of patterns. An illustration describing the subconscious
is a beef stew. In a beef stew you have many varying
ingredients. As they are combined together they flavor
each other. Yet one does not dominate the other. You
can tell whether it's a beef stew, a veal stew or a kidney
stew. You can also tell whether or not there are onions
in it. Everything contributes to the general flavor while
maintaining its own unique taste.

In the subconscious mind are many patterns. These
fixed ideas have been established through the years.
Some you planted deliberately; many of them you unconsciously accepted in childhood. Others come from the

universal race mind. Each pattern in its own way is distinct, yet together they all flavor one another.

The cook tastes her beef stew, and realizing it needs a little more salt, adds it. The salt changes the entire flavor, but it doesn't change the uniqueness of each item in it. Or she thinks it needs a can of tomatoes, and puts that in. Again she has changed its entire flavor, yet each ingredient retains its own flavor. When you give a treatment you place into your subconscious an idea which changes the tone of the entire subconscious, but which may not change the specific pattern for which you gave the treatment. Even as you read this book, you are sending into your subconscious a positive factor which slightly improves the entire area of the subconscious. Sincerely repeated, it eventually gets through to the particular negative pattern for which it is intended and destroys it.

When you treat you are annihilating everything unlike the specific idea of the treatment. Your subconscious mind is in constant change all the time. The tone of it changes, the flavor of it changes. Much of each day the events of your busy life throw into it ideas which aren't very good. Yet you expect five minutes of treatment to counteract the sum total of these negatives. Therefore, if you do not get the result from treatment which you expect, the reason is in the melting pot of your subconscious.

Another factor delaying your demonstration is that you do not take your thought off the material problem long enough to let your good happen. While you treat for three minutes, your mind doesn't think of the problem. Then unknowingly you give yourself the opposite treatment. You think negatively about the condition for an

hour. Yet you wonder why the three minutes of treatment didn't work!

After you give a treatment, do something to vary your
thought. I find that detective stories are good for this.
Divert your attention long enough for your treatment to
do its job. Give the treatment the chance to demonstrate.

Suppose you treat yourself for a cold and two hours
later the cold is worse. Just give yourself another treatment. Your first treatment wasn't a failure. The result
merely indicated the need of further treatment. If you
pay attention to the outer situation, you become confused and ineffective. When you are sick, pay as little
attention as possible to thermometer readings, pulse reports, etc. When you judge by appearances, you delay
your demonstration.

If you are seeing yourself as a sick man or woman, that
is not treatment. Say "God never made a sick man, so I
am not treating a sick man. I affirm that I am a perfect
spiritual being operating in a spiritual universe, governed by a spiritual law. There is absolutely nothing but
God, and God in action in my experience." Each time
you are tempted to dwell on a symptom, say "There is
not a word of truth in it."

You always demonstrate your subconscious. It may not
be pleasant to know you demonstrated yours last week,
but you did. A demonstration is any subconscious pattern which comes to the surface and is experienced. This
process is always going on, it always has and it always
will. Treatment is a technique to direct demonstration,
so that you will produce the experiences you want and
eliminate the ones which are unpleasant. That is the purpose of treatment.

All experience is reported to you through your five

senses and then registers in your subconscious. What the
world believes is not always spiritual or correct. You are
immersed in a universal subconscious mind. In this subconscious mind all people are one. This common subconscious mind contains a great deal of good, but it also
contains certain fixed opinions, fixed beliefs, which seem
true merely because billions of people have been thinking them for thousands of years. These race beliefs are
important for you to know about when you treat.

If you are making a sincere attempt to demonstrate
greater good through treatment you should realize that
there are times when you need to deny race belief. The
entire world expects you to grow old, and that as you
grow older your efficiency will decrease. The world problem of age is becoming more serious yearly, merely because people are accepting it. Today, it is a national
problem. It is in the subconscious because everyone has
always believed he had to grow old and eventually die of
a disease.

I learned years ago to take the words "aged" and "old"
out of my vocabulary and put in their place "mature." I
intend to mature, but I do not intend to grow old. I
intend to have a body that will mature and not be as
energetic thirty-five years from now, but it won't be disintegrating. In treatment you deny this problem of age.

Another race belief is fear, that you have to be afraid.
The only purpose fear has is to indicate an approaching
problem. It is a signal that you should start treatment
and deny every negative symptom.

Still another race belief is that sickness is natural. The
world expects you to be sick. Someday I'd like to make
a study to see how many of the so-called normal children's diseases are caused merely by the expectancy of

the parents. The child is scarcely two months old before the mother fears chickenpox and perhaps a little pink eye. It is an unusual child who doesn't go through some illnesses.

In your subconscious mind are these world beliefs in age, fear and disease. If you don't control your subconscious, it will control you. If I own a dog, I tell the dog what to do. If the dog owns me, then I do what the dog wants me to do. Your subconscious is the same way. You can run it humanly through will power, or you can direct it spiritually through treatment. The direction you give your subconscious through treatment determines the experience you receive.

Through treatment you channel the creative power toward your goal. If you have ever been in a sailboat and it was your job to handle the tiller, you know that when the wind suddenly changes it is rough going. You keep the rudder straight. Because you keep it straight the boat is safe. One minute you use a little pressure, a few seconds later greater pressure, but you keep the rudder controlled.

A little knowledge of treatment is a dangerous thing. The beginner says "Life is wonderful, I will never think another negative thought." That is a mental impossibility on this plane of life. The beginner means what he says. He has set his course. Everything is all right as long as the going is easy. Then serious trouble appears and he is upset because his treatment doesn't work instantly. What he does not realize is that only a consistent maintenance of an over-all constructive mental attitude keeps him on the course he has set. It isn't an instant, moment, five minutes or twenty-five minutes of positive thinking; it is the gradual changing of the total mental attitude. As the mind's attention is changed from fear to faith, from lack to abundance, from any negative to a positive, demonstration after demonstration follows, because there is a law that makes your treatment work.

You live in the eternal now. This instant is the only instant in which you are thinking. Being the only time in which you are aware, it is therefore the only time in which you can erase out of the subconscious what you don't want. It is also the only time in which you can place in the subconscious what you want demonstrated. This unconscious part of you, which is the creative part of you, always works in the present, and it always works according to the motivating idea of the present.

To treat successfully, you must learn to think the idea in the present that you want in the future. Doing this will automatically delete from the past all that is not in accordance with your desire. It will also automatically produce in the future the idea you are now declaring in the present.

If today you are feeling on top of the world, your body is well, your mind is inspired and you believe that all things are going to work together for good, you are presenting to your subconscious a positive motivating idea. As that idea goes deep within you, it automatically silences the negative memories of the past and erases the fears of the future. It establishes a pattern for the future and directs a mental process to produce your good.

If you worry today, you reap confusion tomorrow. Confusion in the present accepted by you dominates your thinking, and creates another cause. This cause brings forth an additional effect of confusion tomorrow.

When you are ill, you should declare you are well. That

is your only means of setting up a different cause to produce another effect. As long as you believe you are ill, you are maintaining the cause and it continues to project the effect into the future. Sick people without an understanding of treatment begin to improve when their nurses, doctors and families say they are going to get better. Because they accept this, they do get better. Your world delivers to you at every instant what you mentally accept to be true of yourself.

The powerful subconscious stream of thought constantly gives embodiment to what you really believe about yourself. The self which you really believe you are, you glimpse when you're faced with disillusionment or unhappiness. Alone with yourself you think, "This is what I really am. This is the self which the subconscious makes manifest."

"Take therefore no thought for the morrow" and "Let the dead bury their dead." These two correct psychological statements of Jesus are short and clear. They are necessary assumptions if you are to think effectively. Yesterday, as yesterday, does not exist; tomorrow, as tomorrow, does not exist; this split second does exist. Your future is determined by your thinking in this second. Hope and vision are important, but only as they actually condition the present with optimism. They are not important if they are vague and dreamlike. Your future good will appear because its destiny is of God. The only thing that can prevent its appearing is a negative mental action on your part in the present. Through treatment you control all mental and emotional action on your part which diminishes or delays a future good. The individual who is sick in the present can be well in the future, if he can believe he is well in the present. The person in fi-

nancial trouble can have security in the future provided
he is capable of believing that he has it in the present.
You must accept in the present what you want in the
future. The present is cause and the future is effect. You
will never experience the effect without thinking the
cause.

There is a mental law of giving and receiving. The
ideas you give to your subconscious today you receive as
facts in your world tomorrow. The easiest way to give
mentally today is through treatment. This is true because
you are using language of the spirit and this awakens a
spiritual power in the subconscious which proceeds to
do the work. Spiritual language sets up an inner creative
flow; it releases a creative power. It sends into the subconscious a creative idea, which works automatically,
producing an effect like unto the cause.

If you want to learn how to treat you should be an
optimist. People often say that I am overly optimistic and
that I refuse to face facts. Yet they fail to understand the
essential premise of this technique. "What things soever
ye desire, when ye pray, believe that ye receive them, and
ye shall have them." You will never have your desires
until you believe that you have them now. To the sick I
say, believe that God is your health at this instant; as you
believe it, health appears. To the unhappy I say, God is
the joy and creative expression of your life now; believe
it and you will experience it. The same is true of lack
and all other negative conditions of life. I am not saying
that a man isn't sick, or that a woman isn't sad, or that
the corporation is not bankrupt. Treatment states at the
instant what you want in the future.

If sympathizing would help, I would weep with you
over your problems. But I know that I would be digging

my own spiritual grave. I would be conditioning my future with trouble. It is my job to treat this split second with spiritual concepts of life, expansion, peace, order, abundance and perfect health. To the degree that you perceive these qualities as God in action in your life at this instant, to that degree will you never be sick, unhappy, in want, and never under a law of contraction and limitation.

Treat yourself in the eternal recurring now. Your future is secure only if you are thinking rightly at this instant. The following statement will help you:

I evolve spiritually in exact ratio to the number of seconds per day that I am thinking rightly, thinking of God, thinking of good.

5

⌒〇⌒

Treat Yourself to Success

ARE YOU ONE of the millions who work all day to earn enough money to buy enough food to sleep all night in order to work the next day to earn enough, etc., etc.?

Esther Clark was one of these. She arrived in New York City from a small town in Georgia for her annual four weeks leave with pay.

"If I don't get a better job with more money in a larger city, I will go mad," she told me. "I am nothing but a poorly paid machine. The monotony is killing me."

Esther was a government clerk at an Army Base in a town of ten thousand. She lived in a dreary government-supplied apartment of one room, bath, and a kitchen consisting of a hot plate on a shelf. Her anguish included lack of closet space, dull neighbors, and only one movie in town.

"Do you have the courage to make drastic changes in your thinking?" was my first question after hearing her story.

I talked with her for an hour that day. She came back to my office for two more treatments during her stay in

New York. I gave her a planned program for changing her thinking. I showed her how to treat her own mind to erase the monotony pattern and to establish a creative one in its place. I gave her a list of books to read which would maintain her courage after she went home.

Four months later Esther Clark had another equally routine job. But it was on the staff of a New York publishing house. The salary was better and more important to her, she was in a large, vital city to which she responded with joy. A year later, she moved to the editorial staff of an important woman's magazine at a high salary. She has climbed steadily ever since.

How did Esther do this? Any person with courage, who knows what he wants to do, can change his life from failure and monotony to success and creative living.

Everyone is born with a capacity for success. You are born not only with a success ability, but you also have a drive toward it, an emotional need of it. You have the need and the ability to bring success to the surface of mind and make it factual.

Anyone is a success who is aware of himself as a creative person, and can live without too much emotional stress at whatever level his work in life is. You may be a housekeeper, a mother, a millionaire, or you may be a $40,000 a year person. You are a success if you are doing a creative job in life and can live without emotional strain in the economic and social pattern in which you find yourself.

I do not define success on a money basis, or on the basis of genius, as there are fewer geniuses than the world recognizes. Success is not based on grandiose achievement or the applause of the public. The successful individual is creative in his experience, and is at peace within himself while he is creative. If you are doing this, you are successful, and the money you earn is secondary.

Medical and psychological authorities in the last fifty years have awakened to the unity of mind and body. They now write of the mind and body relationship. The day will come when they will expand their vision, experiments and laboratories, and perceive that as the mind can make man's body sick, so can the mind make man's business world sick. They will realize that man, as man, must be everything which he is, and that this everything which he is includes his total experience. A business failure is indicative of man's ignorance of spiritual facts.

A failure is not necessarily a person who is bankrupt. A failure is anyone who, either through his own ignorance, or through his acceptance of situations apparently beyond his control, has resigned himself to some form of expression which is frustrating rather than creative. This causes an emotional conflict in his subconscious mind, producing lack of ease, a sense of guilt, and a feeling of insecurity. This can happen to the man earning a million a year as easily as it can happen to one earning $80,000 a year. Success and failure are not monetarily evaluated. They are judged on the basis of consciousness. That is why every religion has warned you that the only thing you will take with you in death is your mind. You cannot take your success or failure in the world to further existence, but you do take your subconscious with you.

Your consciousness, your thinking-feeling process of life, is what you are. You did not create it, nor can you stop it. You are it. Consciousness is something which you cannot create; you cannot destroy; you can only direct. The entire science of treatment is based upon the premise that the thinking-feeling power in you will follow direction, and will do what it is told to do. The thinking-feeling you, that something in you which caused you to be, can be directed, can be channeled, and it will produce for you the results of your command. By your channeling of power, you produce either a pleasant experience which you call heaven, or an unpleasant experience which you call hell. Each week you have a little heaven, and you have a little hell. You have created some pleasant conditions, and you have created some unpleasant conditions.

The human mind excuses, alibis; and material reasons are manifold. You have your pet excuses. Spiritual geniuses, however, see right through these excuses and alibis of the human mind. They lay bare consciousness as the surgeon can lay bare your heart in surgery. Spiritual teachers say: "In you there is a creative power of mind and emotion. You use it. Behold what you have done with it."

Thought and feeling are one process. The person who is a failure has used that process, and the success person has used the same process. There is not a process of failure in contra-distinction to a process of success. There is one process, and you direct it. There is one way of reacting to life, and you channel it. What you decide must through a law of mind appear. There is a law of cause and effect, sowing and reaping. This is the law of life.

If there are laws of chemistry, physics and other sciences, then there are laws of mind and emotion. A science is based on a hypothesis, a principle, and a law of action. Otherwise it is not a science; it is a philosophy. Treatment is a science. I am teaching a law, a principle and a technique.

The failure person uses the same amount of energy as does the success person. When you are completely bored, you are using energy at a tremendous rate. It takes energy to be bored. It takes energy to be unhappy. Gloom, depression and fear are enormous energy users. They are directions of the stream of life into negative patterns. Law which is basic must produce after its own kind. The sick become sicker, the unhappy become more desolate, the person with his entire attention on "I haven't enough money" receives even less money. The person whose failure consciousness is "No one loves me, no one appreciates me," finds that fewer people will listen to him. You can only produce what you channel, what you direct, what you are.

When you are reduced to spiritual, emotional and economic poverty, you can change that feeling of negation into a positive power.

There is a divine something in you, which at any time you can channel and direct. The next time you are unhappy and depressed, remember that you can stay depressed, or in an instant you can change over to the positive.

Groups who work for the rehabilitation of the individual, whether the Salvation Army, Alcoholics Anonymous, or the Red Cross in disaster zones, have proved beyond the shadow of a doubt that you can change from failure to success. You can even change in a short time from the sorrow that a death may bring to the certainty of knowing that your life can go on as a creative process. The mighty are often brought low, but when they know what to do, they become again the mighty. They use rightly the only thing they have, thought and feeling. They realize that there is no judgement, no condemnation, no hell and no hell fire. They recognize that the infinite spirit, the divine presence and the inner thought are always saying "Be positive."

Arrive at self-understanding, self-evaluation, and self-determination, and you will move out of the pattern of failure, into the pattern of success. People are doing it every day and you can join them as did Esther Clark. There is nothing to hold you back; all of life is urging you on. All techniques, processes and laws cooperate with you. The road is always up. You are now the success which God planned you to be.

Most of you instinctively think of someone else when you read that mental blocks within consciousness bar the way to success. I want you to think about yourself. The center of your life is within you, flowing out from you to the circumference. The circumference you call your world, your experience. Realize, however, that the circumference could not be unless there was a creative center within you. This creative center in the midst of you is called by most religions the Spirit of God. It is self-evident that life arises at the center and moves to the circumference. It is self-evident that in the world of which you are the center, you are the only thinker. Being the only thinker in your world, life at the center of your being, moving out to the circumference of your world, must be operated by a law of your thought.

You should assume the attitude, the mood of success. Having done so, accept it as true, and let it happen. You let it happen by giving yourself a treatment, then taking your thought from it. You do not cause it to happen through the human mind. Each time that your human mind moves into action it will disrupt the flow from the center to the circumference. It will confuse the creative process and cause an obstruction.

Though you dislike to think so, every unpleasant thing that happened to you last week was a result of your own thinking. You did not deliberately plan these events. They came about as a result of either childhood acceptances, youth acceptances, or conditioning by the environment and culture in which you live.

I have known people who had a definite prosperity consciousness for many years, who were able to live comfortably, easily and with freedom. They did not let major money problems bother them. Little negatives of lack, however, crept into their consciousness. Where formerly they looked at the newspapers and said, "Another tax? All right, I'll make more money and pay it," now they sit back and complain, "Another tax? Someone should change the administration."

Gradually they have allowed a negative to build in their minds until it becomes a block to their success. They do this unintentionally and without any deliberate self choice. Negatives appear in their minds because they do not watch the subversive actions of thought.

You may have mental blocks to success, even though you did not choose to have them. You have them because you unconsciously allowed world opinions to come in and tell you an untruth. You can rid yourself of these blocks in the psychiatrist's office or through spiritual treatment. Untold millions of people have healed themselves of mental and emotional problems. There are not enough doctors in the world to account for the number of such people who have healed themselves.

Your grandmother probably healed herself and she

had never heard of psychiatry or spiritual treatment. Your grandmother did it by going to bed for three or four days and having nothing but toast and tea. What did she really do? She relaxed completely for the first time in months. She had the sleep she needed. She took her mind off things to be done, and placed it on the fact that she was resting and relaxing to get well. She became a well person because her thought produced it. She was actually saying to herself, without knowing she was doing it:

> *There is an obstruction in me between the center and the circumference. I am going to relax and again be established in order.*

Use medical techniques if you want to and if you need to. There will always be people who need professional medical help. But also there will be people who are willing to help themselves. You may suddenly realize that the reason you are not what you want to be is because of something in you. Then, you no longer blame conditions outside yourself, the company for which you work, or the political situation in the country today. You realize failure is in your subconscious. That is the only place you can heal it. Quietly say to yourself:

> *This failure is in me. I now erase it. I stop obstructing the spiritual flow from the center to the circumference. I know that the Mind of God, which created me, is in action through me. It cannot be delayed or turned aside.*

You may say Niagara Falls is not running, but if you traveled to see the Falls, you would find that they are still running. No matter what you say, the universe is a spiritual system and the Lord is still running it. The creative process in you, operating from center to circumference, is the way God acts in your life. It knows what to do, how to do it and proceeds to do it, if you will let it.

Treat yourself to success saying:

This power in me knows what to do. Every block in my subconscious is now destroyed by the action of God. The creative process now has full freedom of action in my life.

Silently think that over and over again. Every obstruction in your mentality to the free flowing action of this power is now destroyed and it moves through you easily, normally, naturally, creating new patterns and new experiences.

Treat in that way for five minutes a day and you will see great things happening. Five minutes a day, deny the fact that there is any obstruction in your mind, because your mind and its essential nature are the Mind of God. Being the Mind of God in action, your mind has never been defeated, is not defeated now and never will be. If there be defeat, it is from an interior action of your human mind which is obstructing the process. You remove the obstruction by denying that the obstruction exists, and affirming that the demonstration takes place.

Treat out your concept that you are the way you are because your father was the way he was. Treat out the concept that you cannot do something because your daughter, your son or some other member of your family does not want you to do it. I have seen many an adult in the same bondage he had previously placed on his children. I have seen the law of cause and effect bring it right back into his own experience. He never let his children have fun, and now the children will not let him have fun! When you use the excuse that you are not a success because you were unhappy as a child, or were not raised in the right environment, or did not go to the right school, you really mean that you have an unconsciously created block which needs to be destroyed. Jesus said: "A man's foes shall be they of his own household." You will never have peace while your mind is disturbed, confused,· unhappy and hurt. While your consciousness is brooding over the past, and worrying over the future, peace cannot prevail.

A wise teacher of treatment said that the premise of all correct treatment should be, "Perfect God, Perfect Individual and Perfect Being." At the present time you may not be perfect. Philosophically, you are aware of a perfect God, but you see yourself as imperfect. You see experience around you as imperfect. You cannot move from where you are to where you want to go, by contemplating evil. You cannot grow through the contemplation of negatives. The individual with his or her mind centered on negatives is one who is in the process of contraction and disintegration. You see around you all the time people who are worried, harassed, disturbed, upset, whose feelings have been hurt. They change instantly from outgoing, outgiving creative individuals into withdrawn and disintegrating persons. Each time you worry you are in disintegration. Each time you are constructive, positive and creative, you are integrated and expanded.

The statement, "Perfect God, Perfect Individual and Perfect Being" is a great idea. I don't know when we will prove it as individuals, race, or nation, but I know that we can prove it when we plan to do so. We will never accomplish it until we believe we can. That is why I consistently tell you in this book that though you may not be what you can be, you are growing toward your goal. The way to be what you want to be is to know that you can be it, and to lay out a definite plan of thinking and feeling to become it. Very few people make a planned attempt to improve themselves. They expect it to happen. You have been indoctrinated through the years by Bible quotations that if you were good, then good would happen to you. You have discovered that there are a great many people who, according to Bible standards, are good people, and they seemingly have more troubles than the rest of you who occasionally are not so good. The righteous do not always triumph.

I have discovered that the rules and regulations laid down for the essential goodness and progress of mankind work only when they are interpreted in terms of the inner person, not the outer person.

This idea of mind change, rather than the old idea of body change, is being accepted today by you who evaluate your experience and realize that your own mental attitude determines your experience, because it does.

What did you want to do when you were eighteen? You wanted to be a very great success. Everyone at eighteen does. By the age of thirty you have accumulated a family and responsibilities and you have settled down. That is the most dangerous thing you can do. It is psychologically damaging. You have conformed to the pattern of Westchester, Beverly Hills or Connecticut. You have accepted rather than chosen this pattern. How many times

you have compromised and accepted patterns rather
than selected them! The unguarded mind accepts rather
than selects.

Ninety-nine out of one hundred don't change their
lives, because they cannot overcome their subconscious
patterns. They are convinced of the material situation.
Their excuses and alibis, though sound at the human
mind level, are idiotic at the spiritual level. Every alibi
you make as to why you don't do something creative is
sound at the material level. At the spiritual level, however, it's the babbling of a child. The infinite doesn't
know you're limited. The infinite can't know that you
aren't able to do what you want to do.

The sun shining down on the beach doesn't know
whether it's winter or summer. The sun shines down on
Jones Beach, New York, or Malibu Beach, California,
every day of the year. It doesn't know whether it's July
with a half million bathers on the beach, or whether it's
January with a lonely watchman on the beach. It doesn't
know if there are clouds to prevent its getting through
to the beach. It only knows that under a law it has to
shine. That's all it knows. The infinite creative process
only knows how to give; it doesn't know how to take. It
is the nature of the creative process to release itself. One
of the greatest explanations of God is the statement,
"God so loved the world that he gave . . ." It is the nature
of life to give. It gives without stint. It gives without a law
of comparisons to know whether it's giving more here or
more there.

You exist in a universe that offers itself to you. You
are in it and have an inner something which is like unto
God. This in you is hampered by the psychological structure of your mind and by the physical condition of body.

There is a divine something within you of eternal generosity which is seeking to come out. You now have a working technique, treatment, to release this eternal generosity.

Be aware of yourself as a creative, producing person and you suddenly find that ways, means and processes develop letting that which is inside come out and create good. As this inner you moves out to the infinite, the psychological structure of your mind orientates itself, balances itself, the tensions go and the ease comes. Your body takes on the tone of health; chronic problems of the years slip off your shoulders and you are well and strong. This inner creative thing in you flows out through you to give of itself unto creation. It finds open hands, because all life responds to the individual who is receptive to God.

How do you treat yourself to success? Start at the point where you are. Analysis of your human mind can only reveal what you do, not what mind is. Psychologists are unable to define what mind is, as are medical authorities. They can tell you about the brain, about the way your mind works, but they can't tell you what it is. The reason they can't define mind is that they are frightened to call it God. They would be out of their field if they said that this mind within you which thinks and causes feeling was a spiritual entity.

The most important thing for you to know about your mind is that it can change. The next most important thing to know is that when you accept yourself as a creative individual, the mind goes to work to make you so. This creative process within you acts when you recognize it. Say: "I am the individual that the creative process intended me to be. Therefore, creative ways open before me." You will then know the joy of success and creativity; the joy of giving something to life, and you will in turn receive appreciation. Whatever your goal for success is, know that within you is the capacity to live life creatively, to give something into the world which will be of benefit to you and to others, and to be appreciated for it.

Treat yourself to success, saying:

In God, the one mind, I live, move and have my being. Good alone is present at this instant, and God always knows what to do and how to do it. Therefore there is in me no mental block to my success. There is only the intelligent action of a perfect God. This full action is taking place through me, and bringing to pass my freedom from all untruth.

The past cannot limit me, the present cannot confound me, and the future cannot cause me to fear. God in me, acting through me, is my guarantee of success. I move forward into my expanded good, divinely directed to successful accomplishment. I rejoice in success, for I am success.

6

⌒〇⌒

Treat Yourself to Freedom

"AM I NEUROTIC? Am I laden with guilt feelings? My subconscious must be a mess." Today such anxieties are the
usual questions asked by troubled people of doctors, cler-
gymen and psychologists.

Few of these people can define the very terms they are
using. They banter these words around with seeming
knowledge and often know little or nothing of their
meanings.

Thanks to Freud who made the first scientific investi-
gation of psychological structure, you now know you have
a subconscious mind. To know you have one, and at the
same time to be ignorant of how to control it, has not
advanced you a single step.

The subconscious is not something to be feared. It is
something to be directed consciously for the production
of healthy results. It is not a demon; and it has no negative tendencies inherent in it. If there are negative patterns there, it is because you have without intention
placed them there through the years. But they can always
be changed into positives.

The subconscious mind was discovered by Anton Franz Mesmer and was explained by Freud. It is the basis of all forms of psychotherapy, including spiritual mind therapy. It revealed that man is predominantly a mental and emotional process and not merely a body creature. Man as the operation of mind, rather than as the operation of body, requires a new understanding of the spirit in man.

Your body does not make you do anything wrong. Consciousness determines body. You decide to act and your body proceeds to do what you decide. Your body does not cause you to commit errors. You must want to commit them, either consciously or subconsciously, to have your body accomplish them. Your way of thinking and feeling is your primary problem. Treatment is the adaptation of spiritual principles to psychological techniques giving you help at the only place where you need help, which is in your mind.

The subconscious mind is the principle operation of your life. You are at least ninety per cent subconscious. Everything you do, you do because your subconscious mind does the work. The area of the conscious and the subconscious and the inter-action of the two are the whole cause and continuity of life. What you decide with the conscious mind, you produce with the subconscious mind. When you do not decide an issue with the conscious mind, your subconscious takes the best material it has left over from previous decisions and produces after its own kind.

If you fail to direct your subconscious mind, it produces under a law of averages, and you are a nice, ineffective, sweet person. There are millions of such people.

You ride with them on trains, you see them in your neighborhood; people who are neither good nor bad, but merely average. They don't do anything evil, for they have been warned they would go to hell if they did. They aren't too good because that is an effort. They aren't bad enough to be in hell, and they aren't good enough to be in heaven.

The important factor in your life is never what you are thinking at the instant. It is the sum total of all that you have ever thought. What you are thinking at the instant moves from the conscious mind into the subconscious mind automatically and adds to the sum total. Unless your conscious mind is spiritually activated, it cannot do anything constructive to the subconscious except add to its sum total.

Treatment is a spiritual idea deliberately accepted by the conscious mind, setting into action a law at the subconscious level. Average thinking is not a decisive direction to the subconscious. Treatment is a command to the subconscious to produce a good. Each time you treat, your thought becomes a law of creative action.

From primitive man to the present, people have prayed. They have prayed without knowing they had a conscious or a subconscious mind. As they prayed, more good appeared in their lives. Past generations developed faith in the use of prayer. They depended upon it to get them out of trouble, but they were never certain that it would.

Today there is a science of prayer. It is a deliberate conscious mind selection of a spiritual idea which then automatically becomes a law of mind action in the subconscious.

All life is made of two factors. In the past we have had

the teaching of duality and of plurality. It was said that you could not know light unless you knew darkness, because there would be no contrast. Many schools of philosophy taught that you had to know evil in order to determine good. I believe all life is a dual action, but this dual process in the individual is the interaction of the conscious and subconscious minds. What has been known in the past as the individual's soul, I define as his subconscious mind. What was known as the spirit in man, I define as his conscious mind.

The Bible, the prophets, the messiahs and the saints have told us that when the spirit enters into the soul of man, he is thereby redeemed out of all nations, all creeds and all problems. In other words, when your conscious mind deliberately accepts a creative idea, and delivers it to the subconscious with a sense of authority, the law of the subconscious proceeds to produce in your experience what this idea has ordered done.

I repeat this for emphasis, because it is the essence of treatment. When the conscious mind of the individual deliberately selects a creative idea, and delivers that creative idea to the subconscious, the subconscious mind acts as a law and proceeds to produce the equivalent of that idea in the individual's experience.

Past generations called this prayer. I call it treatment. Either word is good. I happen to prefer the latter. To me the word treatment indicates an action on my part. It indicates a definite mental action taking place. It takes prayer out of the nebulous and brings it into the factual.

The omnipresent God which is the creative power of the universe works in your world automatically. The seed becomes the root, then the stem, and then the flower. But, in the individual, God does not act automatically, because of man's free will. You have the capacity of determination. Many of you have said that you have free will and add "But I can't lose weight." Anyone can lose weight who will choose to drink water and have one toothpick a day. The person who says he cannot lose weight is the person who cannot make up his mind to do it. But he can do it.

The same thing is true of the person who says "I can't change my job." He means that he subconsciously does not want to do so. Another says, "I can't change my environment." Inwardly he means he does not want to make the effort to do it. But, he can do it. There isn't a thing you cannot do if you want to do it. You have free will. Thousands of people have learned treatment, have proved they can overcome disease and have done it. Others still insist they cannot get well. It depends entirely on the individual. You are the only thinker in your mind. You have the right to select any idea, and your subconscious mind will produce the idea you have selected. The universe around you will reshape itself and reform itself for the accommodation of your experience.

Jesus had not only the ability to prove the creative process for himself, he had the ability to do it for others. He could treat in the finest sense of the word. He could subconsciously accept an idea, and the idea demonstrated itself.

Your subconscious mind is the producer of your experience. Your conscious mind is the decider of your experience. Both phases of mind are spiritual processes working together. They are the God process in the individual, and by your use of them, you determine your life. You can awaken out of mental and emotional lethargy and become a person in your own right. Or you can remain in lethargy, be loved, be appreciated, and later be mourned. Life says that you can become what you choose, but only when you choose it, and are willing to go through the necessary mental changes to be it. That you can do, and that I have faith you are going to do.

A woman came to me in great distress. She had been to a psychiatrist about her husband's drinking problem. The psychiatrist had asked, "How old is your husband?" She told him fifty-five years.

"Psychotherapy cannot change the patterns of anyone over fifty," the doctor answered.

I told the wife she should deny this immediately, and that we would deny it together. It is my firm conviction after twenty years of teaching treatment that the subconscious can always be changed, at ninety as well as at nineteen. The reason the psychiatrists cannot change a subconscious pattern after fifty is that they believe they cannot. Whatever they, you or I believe, is demonstrated in practice.

Actually the essence of this new spiritual therapy is that you can change your subconscious pattern. It is not simple. It is not easy, for subconscious patterns have been with you a long time. Your subconscious is the sum total of all you have ever thought or felt. It is not the momentary denials and affirmations of treatment that are going to change your subconscious. It is the steady impression you give to it, day after day. Whether or not you are aware of it, you are still directing the subconscious when you are not treating.

The greatest single thing you can learn from this book is that you can change your subconscious through treatment and through changing your overall mental attitude you can change your life for the better.

It has been proved not only through treatment but through such successful rehabilitation efforts as Alcoholics Anonymous that the individual's subconscious patterns can be changed at any age. In that organization are millions of men and women, whose subconscious search for oblivion through the abuse of alcohol has been changed to a subconscious desire for life and awareness of new possibilities. This has been accomplished not through human mind therapy, but through spiritual therapy, the belief in what they call a "power greater than themselves."

If victims of the dread disease of alcoholism can change their subconscious patterns, surely you, who have less serious problems in your behavior patterns, can change them. Here is how you do it.

Suppose you are a chronic worrier. Worry is attention on a negative idea backed up with an emotional response. Every time you worry you are giving yourself an unconscious negative treatment. The law of mind does not know if you are treating consciously or unconsciously. It can only do what it is told to do.

It is of no value for the world to tell you not to worry. You have the worry habit just as you have a work habit, eating habit and reading habit. I would be foolish to tell you to "change your thought," because you don't change it that way. How many of you when in great trouble have had loving friends and dear relatives say, "Don't think about that any more, just think about something else. You have done your best." They may even say "Get out and go to a movie." You went to the movie, and all the time you were there, you were emotionally reliving your grief, and no great film star was able to change your consciousness.

The reason you couldn't change your consciousness, was that you had, over a period of days, set up an emotional thought pattern, which governed your thinking and would continue to govern it until you made a depth change. The way to change that pattern is through specific treatment.

Every instant that you watch your thought, deny the negative out of your mind, and think of the positive, you have permanently improved your consciousness. Treatment for fifteen minutes a day is not enough. You must maintain a consistent, constructive overall attitude if you wish to change the subconscious mind. It is a discipline you must maintain until it becomes automatic.

The worriers have a habit of worrying and they no longer worry because they want to worry. You know people who worry all the time; they have a pattern of worry in their subconscious and it is going to continue there until they do something about it. The something they can do is treatment and watching thought. I call treatment mind surgery. It is the way in which you go into the subconscious, destroy old patterns and instill new ones. This may not be instantaneous, but it can be done.

Take the person who is worried over money and the future. Though you may assure him that everything is going to be all right, he goes right on worrying. The first step in stopping worry is to admit that you have the habit pattern of worry, just as members of Alcoholics Anonymous must admit they have a drink addiction. If you will admit that you have the habit of worry you have started on the road to recovery.

Say to yourself:

I am now going to delete and destroy my pattern of worry out of my consciousness. I know that my mind is a center of divine operation. I know that the intelligence of this universe, which is God, created me to be in this universe a thinking, feeling, vital being. The intelligence which created me, sustains me, watches over me, takes care of me. I am aware that the mind of God is in action in me and through me as I direct my attention to it. The pattern of worry, the pattern of negation, I now annihilate. The mind of God now operating in my thought has destroyed this negative. It is finished, and in its place is a divine positive. I accept this universe as it really is. This universe is a wonderful place.

People come to my office worried and upset. They are fearful over something that might happen, perhaps did happen. They come in with the feeling that nothing is worthwhile any more. I say to them:

"You have been on this planet a number of years. I doubt very much if during all these years you have really been poor. You look as though you always landed on your feet. Somehow or other, things have always turned out all right in the long run."

Why not think this way:

I've lived to my present age. I've always had enough to eat, I've always had garments to wear. I've always managed to get by one way or another. The power which sustained me to this point is operating in me at this instant. The mind which brought me this far takes me the rest of the way. Therefore, I say to this fear pattern, "Get thee behind me, Satan; get out of my consciousness; you are no longer a part of me." I now give my full

attention to a positive, creative, dynamic idea of God. My uni-
verse is a mathematically correct system, a spiritual system. It
maintains me as I get out of my own way.

Let's say you have given yourself this treatment. Twenty
minutes later you begin to worry all over again. That
happens to everyone. You have been disturbed, you gave
yourself a treatment, you feel better—and twenty minutes later the worry returns. It returns because the subconscious pattern is still there. This pattern, like anything
else, you have to chip away gradually. You do not clean
your whole apartment at one time. You start with the
bedroom or the living room, and you work at it until it
is finally done. You have to start at a specific point and
go through to a conclusion. The same thing is true of
destroying negative patterns in the subconscious. It is
not accomplished quickly; it is not done instantaneously.
It is a gradual disciplining of thought, with a consistent
denial of the pattern, and a consistent affirmation of the
way you want it. You cannot conceive that the infinite
mind created you for the purpose of worry. If you do
worry, you are going against the basic law of the universe.

Though you may say the pattern is the result of your
childhood conditioning, environmental factors or hered-
itary traits, I still insist that the infinite spirit could not
create a worrier. It created man, made in its own image
and likeness.

You know many people who are gossips. They do not
even realize they are. If you were to mention this to them,
they would be insulted. "I never talk about anyone,
but . . . ," and then they start. Many people are malicious

and vicious with their tongues, and they don't even know it. I have an acquaintance who has a vicious sense of humor. His style of humor is to make unconscious jibes at someone else. As a result, people shun him and he doesn't know why.

Examine your subconscious as it rises to the surface and see if such false patterns might be in you. If you don't know what your inner negatives are, seek help and find them out. Make your intentions clear in your conscious mind. The more uncluttered your conscious mind, the more power you can direct to the subconscious. Make a friend of your subconscious. The more you praise the subconscious, the more it produces good for you.

Your subconscious is your area of use of the universal subconscious which is God, and God loves appreciation. God responds to recognition. The subconscious mind will be to you exactly what you believe it to be. If you believe in an unjust, unloving God, you will get what you believe. If you see Him as an all-loving power, He will respond to you as that. To the bitter, God is bitter. To the loving, God is loving. Treat your subconscious with esteem and praise. Treatment sows the seed, the law of the subconscious provides the harvest. Your consistent, positive attitude gives the seed time to grow. Sow it, forget about it, and let it grow. This is the creative process of treatment. It is as simple as when you open the refrigerator door and say, "What will I have for dinner?" The food in the refrigerator does not say "Take me." You put the food in a pan, apply heat, and by a law it becomes cooked. It can't tell you it won't get in the pan. You put it in the pan; you decide this because you are a conscious intelligence, acting upon a subconscious form.

If you can stand in front of your refrigerator door and

determine your dinner, then you can do exactly the same thing in any other phase of life.

The consistent education of the general public by psychologists in the last fifty years has made more people know how the human mind works than ever before in history. Yet, millions still make the age-old complaints, "God made me sick," and "Oh, Lord, do come down and put your hands upon me and heal me." The psychologists are throwing the individual within himself to solve his own problems. And that is exactly what the Bible says you have to do. There isn't a God who is going to come down from somewhere to you and change you.

You must change yourself by acting upon your mind consciously the way you want your world to react to you subconsciously. You do not invoke the power of God, because it is already in you. It does not need to be asked for, because it has already given of itself to you. You are in a spiritual universe to act, decide, select, and upon your decision rests your experience.

Many think that the way to treat yourself to freedom, to joy in your subconscious, is to have a change of scenery, or a change of environment. You think you'll feel better if you go to Florida or California. Remember that when you leave your present place for greener fields, you are taking yourself with you. That is the thing I always think about when I go on a trip. I say: "Barker, the only thing you are taking on this trip, outside of too much luggage, is yourself." The you that leaves your home town is with you every step of the way.

Change of scenery does not guarantee your improvement. Improvement takes place only when there has been a clarification at the subconscious level of mind. You improve in exact ratio to the extent of your clarification of your subconscious mind. That is the only gauge, the only standard. That is why treatment is a therapy to be used at the subconscious level of mind. I am not attempting to mold patterns for people, or make them replicas of piety or virtue. I am always suspicious of the person who looks too virtuous, because he has had to work hard to be it. I am never suspicious of the person who is free and open, of the person who can laugh with ease, cry with ease, and participates in life with ease. Such a person is capable of taking in and giving out creative ideas. He is the one who is the hope of the world.

In you there is a center where you are still an uncluttered person. At the center of you, deep down under all the layers that have been put upon it, is a clarity of life, which is seeking normal and perfect expression. Back of a neurosis is that which is never neurotic. The neurosis is the temporary covering which has been placed over that essence of life which is seeking to express itself normally. Just as your shoe covers your foot, but the foot is within it.

Back of your problem is something which remains untouched and untroubled. In the midst of confusion is something which is undisturbed. Within you at the center is the God-Idea in you. Treatment starts at this center and works up through the many coverings. You are not trying to go down into your mind and break the subconscious layers. You start with the fact that at the center there is that which is true. It is not only true; it is all power; it is all intelligence; it is all life and it is all good. By your recognition of it, it is quickened into action. It needs no pressurizing; it merely needs your belief in it.

When Jesus stood before a sick man, he believed that

there was a well man within the sick man. Because he believed there was a well man in the sick man, his belief uncovered the well man and the sick man disappeared. Jesus did not put health into the man. Jesus did not apply it from the outside. Jesus did not prescribe; Jesus revealed.

Your good, your joy, your happiness starts at the center of you, comes up through the layers of patterns in the subconscious mind, comes through to the surface in a creative and valuable way upon your recognition of it, and upon your demand that it shall be done. Jesus told his disciples that he had come that their joy might be full. Jesus knew as does modern psychology that ideas abiding in the subconscious mind, causing patterns, are the way that life really is. He said, in effect, if my constructive ideas are embodied in your subconscious mind, then the work that I have come to do is accomplished. I came that your joy might be full, and the only way that your joy can be full is when great creative urges, desires, inspirations and hopes deep within you are coming out through you into creative self-expression with a feeling of accomplishment.

The process of treatment is one of deletion of the negatives. Your subconscious mind already has a divine pattern in it of what you ought to be. Being there, you do not have to pray to have it. You do have to treat to be rid of the idea that it isn't there. In a treatment for prosperity, you treat your subconscious mind that there is no negative belief causing you to owe one cent, because God is your infinite supply.

If I believed what the people told me in my office, I couldn't help them. While I am listening to them, I say to myself, "There isn't a word of truth in it." I don't tell the individual this, for he is the one experiencing the pain, the discomfort, or the inharmony. I listen to him, but I do not become involved in it, because it really isn't so. The moment I recognize the problem as factual, I can't help the patient.

There is nothing in psychotherapy which starts with man's basic, perfect pattern. It does not include the basic pattern of you in the subconscious, which in the Bible is called the Son of God, the "I Am," the Christ. This pattern is there, and the reason that treatment is successful is because it is there. You are not rearranging patterns in mind, you are uncovering and revealing the basic, perfect pattern which God placed in you of yourself.

Through treatment, the divine pattern comes to the surface. As it comes to your conscious mind, it causes you to expand and rejoice in good. You change from the pessimist to the optimist because you have lost your old patterns and found your new ones. This is the new birth. You are no longer putting new wine in old bottles. You have only the new wine of life in the new cask and you are vital and fresh. Say to yourself:

I believe that at the center of my being there is a power which is a joyous, creative power. I believe that my recognition of this power causes it to act for me. I now recognize it and say, come forth; break through every obstruction with which time, space and memory have surrounded you. Break through every pattern of the I can't, or the I shouldn't, or what will happen if I do. Break through the past of background, heredity, and tradition. Joy in me, come out through me, in creative ways of good, unrestricted by my own memory and my own background. Come out and operate through me. There is a joy at the center of my being. This joy I did not create, but it created me. This joy in me is spiritual power. I now release it. Nothing in me blocks it. I let it out and it finds creative ways to appear. It makes me a whole and better person. It takes me out of what I am not, into what I really am, and into what I want to do and will do.

7

⌒⌒

Treat Yourself to Life

"HEALTH, HAPPINESS AND Prosperity" is the modern car-
rot held in front of the hungry donkey, hoping he will
haul away the cart of human troubles. Exaggerated promises bombard you on all sides. Your radio promises them
through breakfast foods; magazines offer them through
beauty and charm advertisements. Even pseudo-psychological and philosophical systems have been created to
suggest your immediate change into a glamorous, wealthy
and successful person.

None of the above systems mentions that to live life
with some degree of success inner changes are necessary.
They merely offer to put a new slip cover on the same
tired, old davenport.

Your life is all that you really have. Your years on this
planet are your most priceless possession. It is perfectly
normal to want health, peace of mind, security and creative self-expression. You would be a strange person not
to want these things. But you'll never secure them from
the outside.

The only security you have in this world is the handling of your own thought. Your insurance policies will give you a decent burial and leave a bit more to your heirs. But, your mind alone determines your experience while you are here on earth.

Your friends, the newspapers, and the pseudo-psychological and philosophical systems will gladly tell you how to get health, happiness and prosperity. In the material world you get what you want by fighting for it, by working hard for it, through sheer force, pressure and demand. Many people are very successful on that premise. I can't say that this doesn't work, because it does work. I have seen too many cases of people who became successful because they decided to; they worked hard to become so, and they often worked long hours far into the night. Their interest and enthusiasm were to that end, and they produced what they wanted. There must, however, be an easier way. While these people are pushing, demanding and pressurizing, there are quite a few successes who go far and do not push or demand. They quietly and easily go up the ladder and arrive at the top. Their health remains good, their way of living is easy, and they find that they are on top without having to use the pressure method.

If there is such a thing as a spiritual principle, it must be in all, through all and in action by means of all. Whether the individual is good or bad, right or wrong, on either side of the political fence, he is using a spiritual principal. But most people don't know that they are using it. Quite often they will say to me:

"My husband, grandmother or my mother did unconsciously what you are now teaching me to do consciously. They didn't even know they were doing it. They just lived that way."

There are a great many people who unconsciously use this spiritual technique, but if you told them they did, they would chase you out of the house. Many business men and women use spiritual principles in their offices, but if you were to tell them that, they would be indignant. Unfortunately, the word "spiritual" today has a rather unpopular meaning. It is confused with piety. I do not discuss piety because I do not indulge in it. I do use a spiritual principle of life. The spiritual principle of life is founded on the acceptance that there is a God. This God must be in its creation, and so it is in me. In me, it must be my area of thought and feeling. By my recognition of it, I direct it.

Can you have health, happiness and prosperity through a spiritual technique? You know how to get it the other way through pressure. Many have made remarkable successes through using the spiritual principle. Right away I think of that quiet, simple man, Jesus, who was a success in life. He was a greater success in life than he was in death. The orthodoxy which has been built upon his instruction has been a death instruction. A reader may ask "Don't you believe that Jesus died on the cross for me?" No, I don't believe it, but you have a perfect right to believe it. I believe that his life was a magnificent illustration of how to get what you want through using a law of mind action. Naturally, when you get what you want through a spiritual technique the world won't like it too well. All the pushers and the high pressure people will be annoyed because you do it so easily while they work so hard.

People who come to me for consultation want prosperity, and an increase of good in their lives. Inevitably they tell me that they work too hard for their money. I immediately say:

"What are you working for? If you are working only for money, there is no sense of your studying this teaching. When you study along this line of thought, you no longer work for money, you work because of a need for self-expression, and money happens, but it is a secondary interest."

Jesus was destroyed by the people who didn't like the way he did things. The high-pressure people had him killed. During the three active years of his teaching and producing results, he said often, in effect, you are going to believe something. He discarded the force, the pressure and the demands which other leaders of religion used.

Jesus implied you do not live the usual material way; you merely believe something. The public answer was: Nonsense; we must organize an army, we must get rid of these Romans, we must lower the taxes, and certainly we must finish rebuilding our Temple. Jesus' quiet answer was to the effect: No; all you do is believe in yourself as God-created. Naturally the crowds didn't stay with him. They didn't want to change their belief. It was easier to recruit an army, as it is today, than to think justice, order and harmony about your fellowman. They didn't want to believe a new idea; they wanted to act upon an old one.

We all want to do something definite, but we shy away from believing a new idea. Jesus taught a principle of success premised on a law of belief, and a very simple law it was. If you believe it, you have it. This is so simple that it immediately strikes your intellect and it bounces back. "That can't be so; it is too simple." So his followers took this simple idea and made it complicated. They split it up into three ideas and built a church structure around it. Next came theologians, who could argue about how many angels there were in heaven, and how many devils there were in hell.

This crucified the simple teaching of Jesus. Read the Four Gospels and note the times where Jesus said "Do you believe?" or "Do you have faith that this can be done?" He was constantly saying to people, "Do you believe?" When they replied that they did believe, he answered "Then it is done." They reasoned this couldn't be, yet they realized they had been instantly healed. It had been done. They still could not realize that it was not a miracle, that it was the law of acceptance and the law of belief; it was merely a spiritual use of mind, a spiritual use of consciousness.

I have given this instruction for fifty years. I see mind and its action, consciousness, as the real person. The real you is your consciousness, it is your use of mind. Your consciousness includes both the conscious and subconscious action of mind. The real you is your use of mind, not your body. Your body has been changing constantly since the day you were born. Nor are you the world about you for that also is changing all the time. You are mind in action; you are feeling and thinking; you are consciousness. Jesus knew this and he was able to do things which the people who didn't know it couldn't do.

When you know a science which others don't know you can do things they can't do. I don't know how to play the piano. I hear others play and enjoy them. I don't know how to play, so I can't play. They know how to play, so they can play. Jesus did something which anyone can do. He did things which other people couldn't do at that instant; and because they couldn't do them, they assumed they never could do them, and so they never tried to do them.

Treatment is so simple that you don't think you can do it, and because you don't think you can do it, you don't try it. Yet ever since the time of Jesus, people have been doing it unconsciously and a few people have done it consciously.

Treat yourself to greater life. Don't assume that you can't do it or that it requires piety or theology. Assume that you can do it, and then proceed to do it. There is nothing difficult about treatment. All it asks is that you try. The beginner fumbles in any science. You will for some time be inaccurate, because that goes with learning any science. Later you become disciplined to the technique of treatment; you use it and you have results.

If your mind is able to project far enough ahead, casting aside all that your human mind will tell you cannot be done, you will realize that you can do it. In your own consciousness say:

I know what I want in my world. I am now going to believe that I have it.

Your human mind argues "Yes, but you don't have it. Your chances of getting what you want are very slight. You are getting too old to have it. With prices of everything going up, it's going to be harder to get what you want."

You have humanly argued yourself out of more good than you will ever know. You have argued yourself out of untold good that could be yours by letting the outer mind describe all the reasons why it couldn't be done. Can you believe that you already have your heart's desire? That is the essence of treatment. If you believe that you have it, it happens; but it can't happen until you believe that you have it.

A word of warning. Don't talk about treatment and demonstration to other people. They are incapable of believing it. A friend came to my office and told me of the complete disappearance of a cancer in its advanced stages through his own spiritual and mental treatment. He treated himself. It had been correctly diagnosed as cancer by the medical profession, and it disappeared. It disappeared in a matter of thirty six to forty hours after he had treated it. Some of you readers will say "I don't believe it." You have a perfect right to say that. You are honest. But there are a great many people in this country and in the world today who know that it is so.

I have told my mind to be still and be assured more than I have ever said it to thousands of groups which I have addressed. I constantly say to my human mind "Be still, the limitation is not true. There is not one word of truth in it. It is not so." My human mind likes to disagree with spiritual ideas the same as your mind does. It tells me "You can't. You are too old. You shouldn't. What will people think? It's too expensive." I then say to myself "Stop, be still. I have accepted what I believe and it will happen."

Every successful person in any field believed in himself, accepted the fact he could do it and then proceeded to do it. Many of these successful people used the pressure method, but others used spiritual techniques similar to this. In their simplicity these latter people made their demonstration. Treat yourself to life without using the pressure method. Relax and say:

I can do this thing. I'm going to do it in the way of truth. I now believe it. I now accept it. I now act as though it were done and I now let the law of mind do it.

To my human mind I say:

Be still, keep out of the way, don't confuse me, I am working with a spiritual idea, and I will have my demonstration. The infinite responds to the finite, in the terms of the finite. God responds to me in my terms.

The only obstacle to treating yourself to life at this instant is your own thought, and fear is the greatest obstacle to your mental growth. Replace it with faith through consistent treating and you will become what you wish to be.

In the last eighty years psychology has moved fear from the realm of the universal into the realm of the individual. In the older religions, you were afraid of God. In the newer psychological teaching you are afraid of yourself. When fear of God was taken out of religion, the fear of yourself was put in your mind. You are not afraid of God anymore, but you are afraid that you might be neurotic. Historically, a great step forward has been made. Now we have placed fear at the only place where it exists and that is in the human mind. There is no fear on a universal scale; there is only fear at one place, in the midst of your own consciousness. That is where it begins and that is where it ends. Your mind is its sole means of operation, its sole means of continuity, and its sole means of ending. You are no longer afraid of life after death. You are no longer afraid of God in the present. Ask yourself "Where is there a fear in my world?" You soon realize that fear exists only in your consciousness. It still remains a serious problem. It is a subconscious pattern of negation which you have accepted as being authority. Fear is a subconscious authority which you have unconsciously allowed to be imposed upon yourself. As you analyze the situation of which you are afraid, you are afraid of your own thought! You are afraid of your own reactions to life. You are afraid of your own inabilities and your sense of being insecure. You are actually not afraid of a situation, thing or person. You are afraid of yourself. Evil is neither person, place nor thing; it is your interpretation of life from a negative viewpoint. The moment you examine the evil in any situation and perceive it as an idea, you have found your first key to overcoming it. You are not overcoming people or places; you are overcoming a belief in your own consciousness.

With friends tonight you may discuss world conditions. The first thing you know you are almost ready to sell all the securities you have. You become depressed and unhappy because you have allowed a negative atmosphere of consciousness around you to reaffirm the negatives in your own subconscious, and your individual fears come to the surface.

After reading this book you will see fear for what it really is. Say to yourself "Why should I allow the negative thinking of my friends to make me depressed?" Listen to your friends and appreciate them, but do not let them enter your mind and confuse you. You are then handling fear in your own consciousness. The greater portion of the people in the world today are afraid of the future. I trust that you are not among them, but if you are it is time that you came out from among them.

When you know your consciousness is cause and your

world is effect, you begin to view your panorama of life quite differently. The widespread fears of insecurity in the future need not be in your pattern, need not affect you. Why allow this to come in and dominate you? Say to yourself:

I refuse to be upset by speculations of fear. If other people want to worry about the next war, I still will expect permanent peace. I will live in peace and with the people in my own apartment house. That is one of my contributions to world peace.

If every person reading this book would live in peace with his own family and with the people in his own neighborhood, he would be a true peacemaker. Peace, like fear, begins and ends in your own consciousness.

Psychologists imply that fear is a subjective pattern which needs to be examined, revealed and self-seen in order for it to be clarified.

You can do this without exhaustive psychoanalysis. You can do it by a power which through the years has been called faith. Fear is faith in reverse. A fearful person has faith in a negative. The cause of any fear is a negative emotional reaction on your part. It was not the situation which caused the fear; it was your reaction. Refuse to react to a negative; react only to a positive. Say to yourself:

Whatever pattern in my subconscious is causing me to have this sense of fear and frustration, I now erase it by this word of truth which I am declaring. I establish in its place the opposite, which is a sense of security and order.

Have faith instead of fear. You are going to do this by building your spiritual ego. You do it by affirming your faith in yourself. You have faith in many other things; you will now have faith in yourself. You will believe that the evolutionary process which has brought you this far on the road of life, will carry you the rest of the way. Life will continuously evolve you; life will continue to make you grow; God will continue to give you a universe ever-expanding in possibility. You can believe that.

Faith is a positive attitude developed as a result of making affirmative statements in mind, whether they are religious statements or not. You have faith in a business. Many of you have faith in a pet department store. That is the store where you feel at home, where you never had any difficulty, where you can return any purchase and always have your money returned. If you have faith in a department store, you can have faith about any other situation in your world. You develop faith in God by thinking positively about life in your own mind. You establish faith in anything if you repeat positive thoughts about it. Watch your thought constantly and each time a negative appears, turn it out saying:

This kind of thinking is not right. I am not going to indulge in it. I am going to declare a positive. I have faith in God's universe.

You are in a universe that is eternal so you might as well adjust to it now. You need not worry about the end of the world. You need not fear the insecurity of the future. You need not fear disease or death. You are alive and the universe is alive. You always have been alive and the universe has always been alive. You always will be alive somewhere, and the universe will always be at that point where you will be, for you are in an infinite system which is God in action. You are in this infinite system and it is moving under a law of good and an impulse of right action. It moves under a creative law of production. The universe will continue whether you fear or do not fear, whether you have faith or do not have faith.

The universe is eternity and infinity. Either flow with it, with the faith, "I shall not be afraid, for within me is the Action of God," or you go against it and say "World conditions are terrible." You can live in either world you select. You alone can decide the world in which you are going to live, because it is your world. It is made up on the conclusions of your consciousness. Why not live in it with faith? Jesus used the simple statement, "He that sent me is with me." The mind which sent you is with you. The intelligence which produced your body is still operating through it as life and health. The intelligence of this universe is the intelligence of your business and it can prosper it. The intelligence which created this orderly cosmic system is the order and harmony of your life, if you will live in accordance with it.

Some of you readers may be able to live without fear for twenty-four hours a day, seven days a week. I hope you can. I know that I live with less and less fear all the time. If I live with less fear, I must as a result live with more faith, because fear and faith are the same action of mind, one toward the negative, the other toward the positive. The more that you have the feeling of being supported, maintained and operated by a mind, a power and a presence, that is not your own, the more you are going to have faith. You can go to your psychiatrist for help if you desire that method. You can go to your minister or metaphysical practitioner, if you wish that method. Or, in your own home, you can relax and say:

I am not afraid of any situation, person, place or thing. There- fore, I now declare that in the midst of me is the power and the presence of God sufficient unto every situation. I rise up in the dignity and integrity of myself as a spiritual being, and I know that the power that supports this universe, supports me, and I allow it to do just that.

There is a mixture in you of the good and the not so good. There are times when you act well, behave beau- tifully, love everyone, get along with your neighbors and co-workers. There are also times when you can't agree with anyone. Alone on a shipwrecked island in such a mood you couldn't even agree with yourself.

When science evolved out of the realm of the myste- rious, it began to classify, to accumulate its data, to solid- ify its impressions on a known and reputable basis. It made an extensive study of the individual's past. It was for many years interested in the question "Where did we come from?" Science was unable to believe in the Gen- esis story of man's creation and developed theories and branches of science to explain man's origins. From this came the statement of evolution.

From 1700 to the present, the so-called Scientific Age has studied the past of the individual. It has explained the individual's presence in terms of his or her past. You are what you are because of what the cultures of many races and nationalities have made you. Your own hered- ity and environment became important.

About 1900 there came the science of psychology. With psychology, the scientists began to study the individual in terms of the present. They were interested in how your mind works. They were interested in your emotional responses. They paid less and less attention to the older theories of heredity and environment, and more and more to your present ways of thinking, reacting and emoting. Later, however, they again went to the past and repeated the situation all over again. Today you are once more told by the major schools of psychology that you are the victim of the past; that the first six years have conditioned you, that experiences during those six years determined your drives, motives and the way you direct your life.

The psychologists are perfectly right in what they are saying. But I do not believe that the individual is explained in terms of his or her past, whether it be in terms of evolution, anthropology or psychology. I believe that you can only be explained in terms of your future. As you read the prophecies of the Old Testament, the teachings of Jesus, the writings of Paul, the works of men such as Emerson, Whitman, Browning, Fox, and Ernest Holmes, you discover that these inspired people are all saying one thing. You can become something and your capacity to become is not dependent on what you have been; it is dependent on what you are, and you can improve what you are.

As I understand the teachings of Jesus, after my fifty years in the ministry, he dealt with people as they were at the instant he met them. When they wanted to talk about the past (you know most of us like to) he said your sins are forgiven thee, just don't do it again. He reminded them of the necessity of becoming something greater than they were.

In every one of us is a drive, an impulse, an intuitive

something that says "I can be a better person than I now am."

The term "a better person" I will leave as a general statement and let you interpret it for yourself. Certainly I don't want everyone to be like myself. God's mind didn't intend that any two of us should look alike, act alike or react alike. We are all individuals and have individual experiences and individual reactions to life. That is why any totalitarian system is bound to fall eventually, because it is contrary to the basic nature of the individual. You are supposed to be you. You are not supposed to be a number, an unnamed member of a group. You were created to be an individual expressing yourself. That is why the Lord made you. You are only of value to your universe when you do it. There are many ways of self-expression. I am not saying that you have free license. I am saying that you are in a universe which is created by a spirit, an intelligence and a wisdom, and you are a part of it.

In order to live effectually in this system, you must evolve into something greater than you presently are. All of God is for the man, woman or child who seeks to improve himself. There is nothing in the universe to refute this. There is nothing in the universe which can deny it. All of God is for the individual when the individual behaves himself and moves ahead.

You are only in your right place in life when you are in action. You only assume the responsibility of life when you are projecting something which is creative and valuable to your fellow man and to yourself. Otherwise you might just as well not exist. Untold numbers of people whom you see around you in your working day might just as well not exist. I don't mean that they should be exterminated; I mean they are not making any creative response to life. They awaken, they work, they go to sleep, period. If they go to a movie, they are bored. If you suggest they read a book, they haven't the time. These people are conditioned individuals, hemmed in by a lassitude and passivity which they could break, if they only would. When you awaken to the fact that you are a son of God, that the universal creative process acts through you when you let it act, you will be startled into creative activity.

If I can't look ahead to my remaining years with an expectancy of creative experience, then there is no sense in doing more than getting myself into a nice little rut and a nice little routine. I should work for a corporation that will never cause me to resign or fire me. I can work for thirty years, receive my pension and then live in a bungalow in Florida. God never made a passive individual. Jesus said to people who were defeated, unhappy and bitter, "You are the light of the world, let it shine."

The statement "I believe in God" doesn't mean very much, unless you look as though you believed it. Unless the way you walk down the street indicates that you are glad you are alive. The way some people walk causes me to shudder. They walk unhappy. They walk defeated. They walk with the pressures of life upon them. They are only in an endurance contest to see how long they will last. Yet those same people will say, "Oh, yes, I believe in God."

I not only believe in God, I believe you and I exist in an infinite intelligence which directs us to creative outlets. As you affirm this, creative ideas appear in your mind and enlarge your thinking. They increase your creative fields of action, and you become valuable to your world.

The world, whether of science, friendships, family or business, will always think of you in terms of the past. But there is another viewpoint. The universe, which is the creative process of the spirit, thinks of you in terms of the future. With all that science has discovered about how you became what you are, it still doesn't know what you are going to be. Scientists can tell you why you have the type of body you have; they can tell you where in your brain is the center which causes sight, and the center that causes hearing. They can tell you at what period in the evolutionary process these centers were quickened and man first heard and saw, but they cannot tell you of the future. They cannot predict what an evolving man will become. In order to do so they would have to step out of their field of science into spiritual metaphysics.

A true science can only establish facts which are known and tested. Metaphysics, on the other hand, talks about the individual that will be. You may be in your troubles now, but you need not continue in them. You can get out of your problems here and now.

You can always be better than you are. You are conditioned by the present only to the extent that you subjectively accept it.

People came to Jesus with incurable diseases. What did he say to them? "Do you believe I can heal you?" The answer was "Yes." "All right, then you are already healed by your own belief." When they changed belief, they changed experience. He said "Thy faith has made thee whole." If you don't like what you are, if you don't like where you are, whether in work, home, family or social relationships, a change of belief will cause a change of circumstances.

If this law of belief worked 2,000 years ago, it will work

today. You can use alibis and maintain yourself in your present experience. Most people are still at the level where they catch colds because of draughts. We still believe that we get tired because the office is exhausting. No doctor in the psychosomatic or psychiatric field will completely accept these excuses. You get tired because you have a subjective resistance to work. That is what makes you tired. You don't want to work so your body very carefully arranges it so you can leave early.

It is difficult to realize that the thing you want is where you are. All that needs to be done is to correct your belief. Hope has done more to lift the world than all that worry has done to destroy it. Every hour of worry in your experience has not destroyed you, but it has hampered you, limited you and made you sick. It has not destroyed you, however, because within you there is something which hopes. There is something which desires good. There is something in you which your worry can never destroy, but which your faith, your vision and your belief can affirm and thus make you the person you are going to be. Your negatives delay creative action. That is all they do. You are going to be greater anyway and you can speed up the process as you realize that deep within you there is a divine pattern which makes you greater than you are at this moment. Realize that you can treat yourself to life.

Summary

THIS BOOK WAS written to give you a practical spiritual technique for richer living. My hope is that you will use these simple ideas to produce the life you want. Or you can put the book aside, and remain as you are, where you are, getting what you are. Then it will abide in your memory with a million other trivia.

Give to your treatments all the thought and feeling which you formerly gave to your problems. Place your vision on the high ground of what you can be, and I assure you, you will become it. Stay simple. Let go of the complications, the rationalizations and the layers of alibis which your years have sheathed you.

The divine center within you awaits your recognition. You blend with it and with the infinite mind which sustains you through treatment.

Your Guide For Daily Treatment

One.   *Speak aloud all you know about God, the one mind, the infinite spirit.*
For your God and my God is of the living and of the loving.

*Your God and my God pervades all that you think,
feel or do.
God is not to be feared.
God is not negative.
Cast out that concept once and for all.
Give birth to your larger idea of God, the God of the
living, the God of the loving, the God of truth and
beauty.*

Two.   *Having defined God, now declare that you are one
with Him.
All that God is, you are.
You are not a broken fragment of an unknowing,
chaotic universe.
You are a perfect being in a perfect world, an inte-
gral part of perfect mind, of perfect good.
Declare that the divine you has remained untouched,
intact, through all the seeming failures and mistakes
of life.
The divine you has never been sick, poor, unloved or
frustrated.
All that is true of God is true of you.
Repeat this until you are free and at ease in your
knowing of this truth.*

Three.   *Say to yourself that the kingdom of heaven is now,
at this instant, not tomorrow, not next year, but today with all its riches.
Your demonstration of whatsoever you desire and believe is here, now and today.
Do not put off your demonstration through delay,
forebearance and resignation.
Those words are no longer in your vocabulary.*

You are living in the now, and you are demonstrating now, and there are no yesterdays and there are no tomorrows.

Four. *Declare that your fears are as dreams that have slipped away in the light of your new understanding.*

It is done unto you as you believe.

Your faith will make you whole, dissolving once and for all the doubts and fears added unto you, and added to the human race throughout the centuries.

It is done unto you as you believe.

Believe in your good with all your heart and all your mind, which is a part of the universal mind.

There is then no room for fear, doubt or the appearance of evil.

For evil is neither person, place nor thing.

Neither age, disease, poverty nor loneliness are truths.

They are but the warpings, the distortions of your thinking.

You have the faith which is truly yours, and that of the universal spirit.

Five. *Whatever your problem seems at this moment, speak a denial of it.*

Deny each symptom of seeming evil, whether it be in your health, your relationships, your work or your financial affairs.

Affirm with joy in your heart, and with conviction in your mind, and the mind of the universe, that no matter what the problem may seem to be, it is gone, vanished, cast out.

You are now whole.

You are now the total man that God intended you to be.

Your faith has brought the real you into being.

You are an idea in the mind of God.

Treat only your consciousness, never your body, never your work, never your external affairs.

You are a free spiritual being in a free spiritual universe revealing the riches of the heaven of your own mind.

Six.   *Your spoken word now gives to the law that loves you the completed plan of your heart's desire.*

It is the Father within you who doeth the work.

His law now envelops your desire and brings it forth abundantly.

You are now ready to give thanks that you are the perfect you God intended you to be.

You walk forward in joy and peace and gladness, in love and abundance and health, forever and forever in the eternal recurring now.

And it is done.